COLLEGE

1849

EVER ANCIENT, EVER NEW

VILLANOVA UNIVERSITY

1842–1992

THE
DONNING COMPANY
PUBLISHERS

EVER ANCIENT, EVER NEW

VILLANOVA UNIVERSITY

1842–1992

by
David R. Contosta, Ph.D.
and
Reverend Dennis J. Gallagher, O.S.A., Ph.D.

Foreword by
Reverend Neil J. McGettigan, O.S.A., D.Min.

Dustjacket photographs (front and back) by Peter Finger, 1992

The Donning Company/Publishers
184 Business Park Drive, Suite 106
Virginia Beach, Virginia 23462

Steve Mull, General Manager
Richard A. Horwege, Editor
L. J. Wiley, Art Director, Designer
Debra Y. Quesnel, Project Director
Laura D. Humphrey, Project Research Coordinator
Elizabeth B. Bobbitt, Production Editor

Library of Congress Cataloging in Publication Data:

Contosta, David R.
        Ever ancient, ever new / David R. Contosta, Dennis J. Gallagher.
            p.   cm.
        Includes bibliographical references and index.
        ISBN 0-89865-847-0
        1. Villanova University—History.   I. Gallagher, Dennis J. II. Title.
LD5651.V32C66   1992
378.748'14—dc20   92-24373
                                                             CIP

Printed in the United States of America

4

TABLE OF CONTENTS

FOREWORD

"Late have I loved Thee,
O, Thou Beauty ever ancient, ever new,
Late have I loved Thee."
(Saint Augustine of Hippo)

More than sixteen hundred years ago, the great Saint Augustine spoke about the beauty of God in a few words. These words, taken from his *Confessions* (Book X, 27), have excited the minds and imaginations of millions of men and women who have read or heard them throughout the ages.

The beauty which Augustine knew and loved in all created things—sun and stars, earth and seas, flowers and beasts—old and young—led him to that source of all beauty which Augustine called God.

For many graduates remembering their college days, the Villanova experience may have given them a hint of God's beauty. Friendships begun, joys and sorrows shared, wisdom gained through knowledge—these are all parts of that beauty.

Recognized through the ages for his gigantic intellect, Augustine of Hippo has always been equally celebrated for the strength of his passionate desire for understanding. In mind and in heart, Augustine was well beyond the ordinary.

Augustine's inquiring mind and his burning heart are symbolized on the seal of Villanova University. The seal shows a burning heart pierced by an arrow and resting on a book of sacred Scripture. In his garden at Milan, the command, *Tolle Lege, Tolle Lege* ("Take and Read, Take and Read"), came to Augustine as a divine message to seek God in the Scriptures, recalling the moment of his conversion. As he read, these words of Scripture pierced his heart with desire for God, the source of all wisdom and beauty. Taken together, his study of Scripture and his heart's desire for its wisdom symbolize Augustine's life-long search to know and love God.

The search for wisdom and beauty continues in the life of Villanova University. It is its own great beauty, ever ancient, ever new. The words of Villanova's motto proclaim this ultimate ideal of a university education: to discover the meaning of life and the beauty of God in the search for Unity, Truth, and Charity.

Saint Augustine, Bishop of Hippo. This statue stands
watch over the Villanova campus by day and by night.

SAINT THOMAS OF VILLANOVA:
PATRON OF THE UNIVERSITY

"To give treasure away as Thomas of Villanova did,
is the duty of the rich and the privilege of the wise."

Villanova is a word that can stretch its meaning to enfold the unique experience of everyone who knows and loves the university. The name *Villanova*, meaning "new town" or "new house," symbolizes for its students a new beginning. It is a place where ideas and attitudes greet students each year as they set out on a journey of discovery with new teachers and friends.

Some students may know little about Saint Thomas of Villanova, and many know nothing at all. The typical Villanova student knows only that Thomas was the saint who "gave away" his name to the university. Few are aware that he was also a sixteenth-century bishop, Augustinian monk, renowned writer, educator, and scholar.

This ignorance about the patron of Villanova is understandable. It is not important that we know so little about the life and deeds of Saint Thomas of Villanova. What really matters about Saint Thomas is that he was a good and generous man who loved the poor. That spirit of generosity is the same spirit which his name brings to Villanova University.

Pictures of Saint Thomas of Villanova tell that story well. They commonly show the saint of Valencia clutching a bag full of money, treasure which he holds, not to keep, but to give away. For Thomas of Villanova, wealth had only one purpose. It was something he could share with the poor, with those who were in need of it.

That is the enduring value of education at Villanova University. Education means gathering the wealth of wisdom and learning, which students possess not for themselves, but to share with one another and, as Saint Thomas of Villanova did, to share with those who need it.

For 150 years, the Villanova family has shared the adventure of learning. Together, they have gathered a wealth of knowledge-treasures of the mind and golden nuggets of truth.

To give treasure away, as Saint Thomas of Villanova did, is the duty of the rich and the privilege of the wise. Villanovans know that this wealth of learning, like love itself, is a gift which we possess never so much as when we give it away.

Reverend Neil J. McGettigan, O.S.A., D.Min.
1 June 1992

Saint Thomas of Villanova. Standing before the Augustinian
Monastery which bears his name, this statue of Saint Thomas
calls the Villanova community to its mission of charity.

Reverend John P. O'Dwyer, O.S.A., S.T.L., first President
of Villanova College, served from 1843 to 1847 and from
1848 to 1850. (Oil on canvas, apparently unsigned.)
Courtesy of Augustinian Province of Saint Thomas of Villanova

CHAPTER ONE
Beginnings, 1842–1892

On the morning of 13 October 1841 two Augustinian priests, Reverend Patrick E. Moriarty, O.S.A., and Reverend Thomas Kyle, O.S.A., set out from Saint Augustine's Church in Philadelphia for Belle-Air, the country estate of the late John Rudolph, located some ten miles west of the city. There is no record of how they traveled, but they probably took the new Philadelphia and Columbia Railroad, which passed through the northern edge of the Belle-Air grounds. As the train puffed through the rolling countryside, brightened by the first colors of autumn, the two priests must have pondered their bold plan to purchase the Rudolph property. There they intended to establish an Augustinian community and school. They had no idea of the challenges that lay ahead, or of the great university, with its thousands of students and scores of buildings, that would emerge from their venture.

In a very real way their mission had begun nearly fifty years before, in the spring of 1796, when Reverend Matthew Carr, O.S.A., arrived in Philadelphia from Ireland. The following August, Father Carr received permission to create the first Augustinian province in America, with himself as vicar general. That same summer he purchased land at Fourth and Vine streets in Philadelphia and shortly thereafter began the construction of Saint Augustine's Church, raising money through subscriptions from Catholics and Protestants alike. Among his contributors was President George Washington, then residing in the capital city of Philadelphia.

Saint Augustine's flourished as a parish church, but the Augustinian community struggled to maintain itself. At one point there was just one Augustinian in the entire United States, Reverend Michael Hurley, O.S.A., to keep the order alive. When the community decided to purchase the Belle-Air estate in the autumn of 1841 there were only five Augustinians in the country, three in Philadelphia and two in Brooklyn, New York.

The Belle-Air estate had been acquired in 1806 by John Rudolph (1760–1838), a wealthy Catholic merchant from Philadelphia. In the fall of 1841, the property included an attractive two-and-one-half story house (built about 1806), a barn, several outbuildings, and just over 197 acres of land, with orchards, woods, and fields. All was to be offered at a public sale on 14 October. The trip to Belle-Air on the thirteenth by Kyle and Moriarty was thus a preemptive visit. Their offer of $18,000 was accepted by Mrs. Rudolph, who may have sold it to the Augustinians for less than its market value as a gesture of religious devotion. Sometime later the Augustinian community purchased all the furniture and farming utensils for an additional $3,400. Title to the property was formally conveyed to the Augustinians on 5 January 1842, later designated as the founding date of Villanova College and University.

The purchase of agricultural implements demonstrated that the Augustinians

Reverend Patrick E. Moriarty, O.S.A., D.D., was President of Villanova College from 1851 to 1855, and was a renowned Catholic orator. It was Moriarty, who with Reverend Thomas Kyle, O.S.A., made the offer to buy the Belle-Air estate on 13 October 1841. (Oil on canvas by Max Soltmann based on an earlier lithograph by Henry McKeon.) *Courtesy of Augustinian Province of Saint Thomas of Villanova*

Reverend Matthew Carr, O.S.A., S.T.B, was founder of the Augustinian Province in the United States in 1796, first pastor of Saint Augustine's Church in Philadelphia from 1796 to 1820, and first Commissary General from 1796 to 1820. (Fine pastel, apparently unsigned, of late eighteenth century origin.) *Courtesy of Augustinian Province of Saint Thomas of Villanova*

The traditional seal of the Order of Saint Augustine is in the foyer of Falvey Memorial Library.

Old Saint Augustine's Church opened for divine worship on 7 June 1801 and stood at Fourth and Vine streets in Philadelphia. The structure was designed by Nicholas Fitz Maurice Fagan. (Lithograph by Packard and Butler, Philadelphia.) *Courtesy of Villanova University Archives*

planned to farm the land, growing much of their own food and realizing some revenue from selling excess crops. The farm would remain part of the Villanova scene until the early twentieth century and would form a vivid part of student memories for several generations.

Since the Augustinians were so small in number, the province sent Reverend John P. O'Dwyer, O.S.A., to Europe to search for recruits. He returned in the summer of 1843 with Reverend Francis Ashe, O.S.A., and Reverend William Harnett, O.S.A. O'Dwyer was then made superior of the Augustinian community which was gathering on the old Rudolph property. At the same time he became president of the Augustinian college, to be opened shortly on the grounds.

On Saint Augustine's Day, 28 August 1843, O'Dwyer said mass in the Belle-Air parlor and placed the new monastery and college under the patronage of Saint Thomas of Villanova, a sixteenth-century Spanish archbishop and saint. Belle-Air had now become Villanova. Yet the name (without the hyphen) would reemerge in the twentieth century as the name of the Villanova year book (*The Belle Air*), of a student dance (the Belle Air Ball), and of a restaurant in the Connelly Center (the Belle Air Terrace).

Father O'Dwyer wasted no time in opening the new college. Like other religious schools in the United States, whether Catholic or Protestant, Villanova had as its main goal the propagation of the faith. Thus Villanova was both a seminary for training priests and a school for the laity. Educated laymen would provide examples for the faithful and allow Catholics to take important positions in American life. There was also the hope that some lay students would pursue vocations in the Augustinian community. In parallel fashion dozens of other small Catholic (and Protestant) colleges were founded throughout the nineteenth century in hopes that some students would decide to enter the clergy.

The first classes opened at Villanova College on Monday, 18 September 1843, with just seven students in attendance. Shortly thereafter three more arrived. The students, faculty, and college president all lived in the old Belle-Air mansion, the students in the attics, the priests and teachers on the second floor, and the brothers above the kitchen. The parlors served as classrooms, the kitchen as a study hall, and the basement as a refectory (or dining room). Little is known about the curriculum, but it seems to have been rooted in the Greek and Latin classics, mathematics, and philosophy—typical for colleges of the day.

Villanova's first prospectus, published in the *Catholic Herald* in the spring of 1844, assured parents that the college was located in a "highly cultivated and salubrious country." It indicated that students could easily reach Villanova on the Philadelphia and Columbia Railroad (later absorbed by the Pennsylvania Railroad and still later by Conrail/SEPTA). The prospectus might have added, but did not, that

This Mosaic in the foyer of Saint Mary's Hall depicts Saint Augustine's first pastor, Reverend Matthew Carr, O.S.A., S.T.B., greeting George Washington and Commodore John Barry (who were contributors to the building of Saint Augustine's Church), accompanied by aides. Saint Augustine's Church, built in Philadelphia in 1801, is in the background.

Reverend Michael Hurley, O.S.A., D.D., was Commissary General of the American Augustinians from 1820 to 1837, and second pastor of Saint Augustine's Church, Philadelphia from 1820 to1837. The portrait was painted in 1813 by Thomas Sully. (Oil on canvas) *Courtesy of Augustinian Province of Saint Thomas of Villanova*

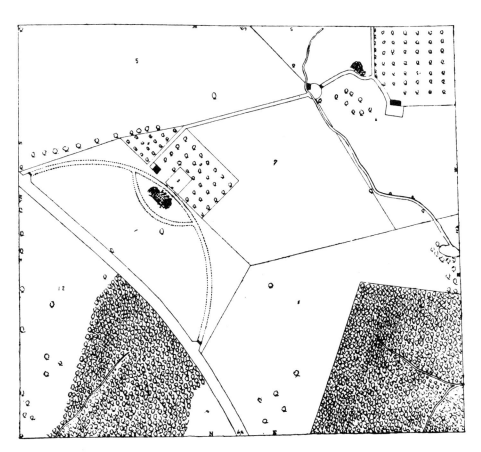

PLATE II —"A PLAN OF BELLE-AIR"—showing (1) the buildings namely, the mansion-house between two willow trees ; a little north-west of it the carriage-house; towards the upper right hand corner, the spring-house, inside a circle ; beyond it, the farm-house shaded by a tree and, near by, a barn ; (2) the carriage drives from the Lancaster Road, and the private ways connecting the buildings and (3) the various divisions of the land in acres, perches and fractions of perches, namely, 1, the lawn (12.61.62) ; 2, garden (0 34.32) ; 3, apple orchard (2.25.50) ; 4, peach orchard (0.96 28) ; 5, field (17 6.70) ; 6, field (16.18.39) ; 7, field (13.5.65) ; 8, field (14 137.93) ; 9, wood-land (11.21.49); 10, field (1.7.60) ; 11, wood-land (8.155.03) ; 12, field (8.18.57) ; then roads (3.18 17) and the total acreage given as 109 acres, 67 perches and 25 hundredths.

This hand-drawn map of "A Plan of Belle-Air," when owned by John Rudolph, was printed in *Historical Sketch of the Augustinian Monastery, College and Mission of St. Thomas of Villanova* (1893), written by Reverend Thomas C. Middleton, O.S.A., D.D. *Courtesy of Villanova University Archives*

This stone pillar represents the campus entrance to Saint Thomas of Villanova Church. *Photograph by Alan Nyiri, 1991*

the Lancaster Turnpike passed through the north side of the property. As a point of clarification, it announced that only Catholics would be admitted, but this rule soon disappeared, and by the 1850s a few Protestant boys were attending the college. Tuition for students over twelve was $125 a year; for students under twelve it was $100.

Given the presence of such young students, it is clear that Villanova College in its earliest years was not an institution of higher learning in the modern sense, but an academy for high school and even elementary school boys. In fact, Villanova would not grant its first bachelor's degree until 1855. By 1893 only seventy-six students had received true college degrees from Villanova. The academy was thus the heart of the institution, functioning as a "feeder" for the college or as a school for boys who had no plans of going further with their educations.

Whether it was a real college or not, Father O'Dwyer began to make improvements to the property during the second year. In the summer of 1844 he added two wings to the barn. These held farm equipment and grain, and provided a crude gymnasium for the boys in bad weather. At the same time, he erected a chapel just west of the old Belle-Air mansion. This house of worship doubled as a dormitory and classroom building for the students, who slept on the upper floors and held their classes and study halls in the ground-floor chapel. Whenever religious services took place, which were attended by students, faculty, and Catholics in the neighborhood,

The Charity of Saint Thomas of Villanova is by the great Spanish painter Bartolomé Esteban Murillo (1617–1682). (Original in the Wallace Collection, London, England.) *Courtesy of Villanova University Archives*

This is Belle-Air, the John Rudolph mansion, as it looked in 1842 when the Augustinians acquired the house and surrounding grounds. *Courtesy of Villanova University Archives*

The 1844 Chapel (demolished in 1902) was used by the Augustinian community, students, and surrounding neighbors. Students also used the building for classes on weekdays. The college bell, visible at left in a locust tree between the former Belle-Air mansion and chapel, called students to classes, meals and religious services for seventy years. *Courtesy of Villanova University Archives*

Saint Augustine's Church at Fourth and Vine streets in Philadelphia was burned during a display of anti-Catholicism on 8 May 1844. The Augustinians of Villanova, fearing a know-nothing onslaught against the college, did sentry duty on the grounds while students vacated the dormitories to sleep off the campus. For almost two years the college was shuttered as a result of the upheaval and its consequences. *Courtesy of Villanova University Archives*

the desks were pushed against the wall and benches were put into place for worship.

Despite such progress the Augustinian community suffered severe losses when anti-Catholic rioters attacked and burned Saint Augustine's Church on the night of 8 May 1844. At first it looked as if the college could go on despite the fire. But the small Augustinian community discovered that it could not run and staff a college at the same time that it tried to raise funds to rebuild Saint Augustine's and cope with the legal complications arising from the riots. Thus on 20 February 1845 Father O'Dwyer announced to some forty-five students that the college would close immediately.

Villanova did not reopen until September 1846. Over the next decade the institution made several gains. On 10 March 1848 the college secured a charter from the Pennsylvania state legislature, which gave it legal standing as a corporation. That same year Villanova began construction of a three-story building (later known as the east wing of Alumni Hall). Designed in the Greek Revival style, it opened in February 1849. The College Building, as it was called for many years, contained dormitories and classrooms, as well as a study hall on the ground floor and a library chamber on the second floor. Meanwhile, Father O'Dwyer erected a small stone railroad station for the college. In 1852 a rear extension was made to the old Belle-Air mansion and the entire structure was raised to a level of three stories.

It also seems that the curriculum was expanding. The college prospectus for 1849–1850 listed as requirements for graduation, "the Greek and Latin languages, History, Geography, . . . Mathematics, Logic, Rhetoric, Poetry, Natural and Moral Philosophy and Chemistry." For an extra $15 per year students could take instruction in the modern languages of French, Spanish, German, and Italian. The prospectus also required students to bring "three suits for winter and three for summer, six shirts, six towels, six handkerchiefs, six pairs of stockings and drawers [i.e., underwear], three pairs of boots or shoes, a cloak or overcoat for winter, and a knife, fork and tablespoon, all marked with his name." Every six months an account of "the health, progress, [and] general conduct" of students would be sent to their parents or guardians.

Although the Augustinians could take pride in a decade of progress, they were

Reverend William Harnett, O.S.A., served as President of Villanova College three times: 1847 to 1848, 1850 to 1851, 1855 to 1857. *Courtesy of Villanova University Archives*

This 1856 photograph shows the enlarged and renovated Belle-Air mansion on the left, the 1848 College Building (Alumni Hall) in the center, and the old Rudolph barn on the right. (Photograph by J. E. M'Clees, Philadelphia.) *Courtesy of Villanova University Archives*

This old spoon was found near the College Building (Alumni Hall) in 1991. *Courtesy of Villanova University Archives*

This two-volume journal was compiled and written by Reverend Thomas Cooke Middleton, O.S.A., D.D. His journals chronicle the life of Villanova College from 1866 to 1923. *Courtesy of Augustinian Provincial Archives*

Monsieur Pierre M. Arnu, A.M., was a graduate of the University of Heidelberg in Germany and a teacher of French and German at Villanova from 1866 to 1903. He left the college in 1903 because of illness and died at Vakke de Zintalapa, Mexico, in 1904. *Courtesy of Villanova University Archives*

forced to close Villanova again in June 1857. The still small community decided that it should concentrate its limited resources on opening up and staffing new parishes in the region, doubtless in response to massive immigration from Ireland over the past ten years. A nationwide financial panic in the late 1850s and then the Civil War forced Villanova to remain closed until September 1865, some five months after General Robert E. Lee's surrender at Appomattox Court House.

The curriculum which greeted the students in the fall of 1865 was little different from the past. Several young priests had joined the teaching staff, including Reverend Thomas C. Middleton, O.S.A., who remained at Villanova until his death fifty-eight years later in 1923. Father Middleton, who would serve as college president and college librarian, also began a journal shortly after his arrival at Villanova in which, for over half a century, he chronicled important events as well as everyday life at the institution. In addition to these Augustinian professors, there were several lay teachers at Villanova in the 1860s. This mixture of lay and religious faculty would remain a permanent feature at Villanova.

New physical improvements began in 1869 when the college erected its first gymnasium, a wooden building eighty-one by forty feet, which stood just west of the 1844 Chapel. It contained "ten-pin alleys, horizontal and inclined ladders, trapezes, a vaulting horse, swinging and parallel bars, climbing pole, bouncing board, breast bars, [and] striking bag. . . ." The gymnasium equipment was dismantled in 1872, however, and the building was converted into a student chapel and parish church for the surrounding Catholic population. The 1844 Chapel became an oratory for the Augustinians.

In 1872 steam heat and gaslights appeared on campus for the first time, and a college post office opened in a new Pennsylvania Railroad station. The next year, in April 1873, construction began on the center and west wings of the College Building (later Alumni Hall), which were occupied for the first time in early 1874. These additions were designed by Edwin F. Durang who would serve as Villanova's architect for the next four decades. The old study hall in the east wing of the building was made into a Dramatic Hall, where several decades of Villanova students gave plays and musical performances.

In 1879 the Augustinians added a fourth floor, with mansard roof, to the old Belle-Air mansion, which now functioned as a monastery and seminary. Far more impressive than any of these improvements was a new college chapel and parish church, begun in 1883 and completed four years later in 1887. Designed in the Victorian Gothic style by Durang, its soaring twin spires would become a local landmark and powerful symbol of Villanova. Upon the completion of this structure, the gymnasium building (which had served as a church since 1872) was reconverted for use as a gymnasium.

The tenor of student life at Villanova during these early decades is unclear. It is certain that students were subjected to rigorous discipline at all times. In the University Archives there are several volumes, known as Jug Books, which list thou-

The Villanova train station continues to serve students today as it did in the past. For many, it represents the first step toward the future. *Photograph by Alan Nyiri, 1991*

Villanova's 1865 faculty posed on the steps of the Augustinian Monastery (former Belle-Air mansion). *Courtesy of Villanova University Archives*

Reverend Ambrose A. Mullen, O.S.A., was President of Villanova College from 1865 to 1869. *Courtesy of Villanova University Archives*

sands of student infractions, the dates on which they were committed, and the punishments exacted. A sampling of misbehavior for 1856 includes "running away from prayers"; "burning fire-crackers in the house"; "drawing obscene pictures in studies"; "throwing snowballs into [the] basement"; "chewing tobacco"; "reading novels in studies"; "stealing eggs"; "bringing a tortoise into the study room"; "using his book for a tambourine"; "throwing Holy Water down another boy's back in chapel"; and "smoking behind the pig-pen." The punishment for this last offense was being "locked up for a day on bread and water." There were several other references to lock-ups and bread-and-water treatment, but it is uncertain whether students were locked in their rooms or in a special cell. In later years punishments were limited to translating a number of lines from Greek or Latin. At no time was there any evidence of corporal punishment.

It also appears that students had very little free time. When they were not taking meals and attending classes, they were required to be in the study hall or in their rooms, with only brief periods to walk, play on the grounds, or exercise in the gymnasium. Daily prayers and Sunday masses were also compulsory. In 1870 the college organized debating and dramatic societies, in addition to a coronet band with eight members. Beginning in the 1860s Villanova students also played baseball. Totally absent were the student dances which would become such a regular part of campus life in the twentieth century.

Villanova brought its first fifty years to a close during the academic year 1892–1893. Father Thomas C. Middleton published a *Historical Sketch of the Augustinian Monastery, College and Mission of St. Thomas of Villanova* in 1893, much of it based upon his copious journal entries. The year ended with a Golden Jubilee Commencement on 21 June 1893, at which Philadelphia's Archbishop Patrick J. Ryan gave the address. The commencement exercises, Father Middleton noted in his journal, took

VILLANOVA COLLEGE,
DELAWARE COUNTY PA.

This institution, under the direction of the Fathers of the Order of St. Augustine, incorporated 1848, with the privileges of a University, is situated in a most healthy and beautiful part of Delaware County, ten miles from Philadelphia; and, being located between the Lancaster Turnpike and Pennsylvania Central Rail Road, both of which pass through its extensive grounds, it is at all times easy of access.

The regular course of studies requisite for graduation comprises the Greek, Latin and English languages; History, Geography, Logic, Rhetoric, Poetry, Ethics, Natural Philosophy, Chemistry, Algebra, Geometry, Trigonometry, and Civil Engineering. When, however, the student is destined to commercial pursuits, or intended to pursue a particular profession, the course of instruction will be adapted to forward his views.

The Collegiate year, which consists of two sessions of five months each, COMMENCES ON THE FIRST MONDAY OF SEPTEMBER AND ENDS ON THE LAST WEDNESDAY OF JUNE.

An ample Gymnasium has been erected on the College grounds, and is at all times accessible to students. Every proper encouragement is given by the Faculty to this and other manly recreations.

All accounts should be paid half-yearly in advance. Students are admitted at any time during the year, and their session commences with the date of their entrance. Should a student leave before the expiration of his session, no deduction will be made, except in cases of sickness or dismissal.

TERMS.

The annual pension for Tuition, Board and Washing, payable half-yearly in advance, is	$250 00
Students who spend their summer vacation at the College are charged, extra,	40 00
Modern Languages, viz., French, German, Spanish and Italian, form a separate charge, each, per annum,	40 00
Music and Drawing at Professors' charges.	
Books and Stationery will be supplied at current prices.	

Each student must, on entering, be provided with a sufficient and suitable quantity of clothing, viz.:—Three suits for winter, three for summer, six shirts, six towels, six handkerchiefs, six pairs of stockings, three pairs of drawers, three undershirts, three pairs of boots or shoes, and a cloak or overcoat for winter,—all marked with his name.

Each student will be required to have a black coat for Sundays and holidays. None of said articles will be furnished by the institution, unless the requisite funds be previously deposited in the hands of the Treasurer.

At the end of the first session a bulletin will be forwarded to parents or guardians, informing them of the health, progress and general conduct of their children or wards.

Communications, etc. for the College should be directed to the President, West Haverford P. O., Delaware County, Pennsylvania.

O. S. A., President.

Villanova College Prospectus, 1872. (Lithograph by Duval Steam Lithograph Company) *Courtesy of Villanova University Archives*

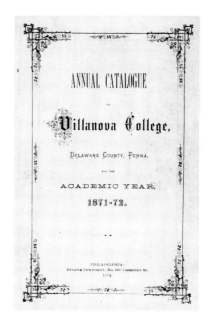

The first Villanova College Catalogue was issued in 1871–1872 under the presidency of Reverend Patrick A. Stanton, O.S.A., D.D. It lists a faculty of sixteen, in addition to three disciplinarians and a visiting physician. *Courtesy of Villanova University Archives*

Reverend Patrick A. Stanton, O.S.A., D.D., was President of Villanova College from 1869 to 1872. *Courtesy of Villanova University Archives*

place in a tent measuring one hundred by forty feet, which was erected in front of the College Building (Alumni Hall). The building and grounds were colorfully decorated in Papal colors, American flags, and red, white, and blue bunting.

Despite its two closings, which amounted to nearly nine years in all, Villanova College had endured to celebrate its Golden Jubilee. Yet it was still a small institution, with only ninety students at the end of its jubilee year, fifteen of them seminarians and seventy-five of them lay students, the majority of whom were academy boys. The years of Villanova's great expansion were still far in the future.

This view of the College Building probably dates from the 1870s (after the center and west wings were completed). In 1920 it was remodeled and named Alumni Hall as a gesture of gratitude to Villanova alumni whose donations had made the renovations possible. *Courtesy of Villanova University Archives*

The bronze-covered dome and gilded cross on Alumni Hall command attention and inspire admiration. The east wing is the oldest remaining structure on the Villanova campus. The west wing was completed in 1874. For many years it was the main College Building and the site of Saint Nicholas of Tolentine Academy, a preparatory school operated by the Augustinians. *Photograph by Kelly & Massa, 1992*

The completion of the center and west wings of the College Building in 1874 allowed Villanova to install this Dramatic Hall (or Assembly Room) in the older east wing of the same building. The space had earlier served as a study hall. It was decorated with paintings of Saint Augustine, Saint Monica, and Saint Thomas of Villanova. *Courtesy of Villanova University Archives*

The twin spires of Saint Thomas of Villanova Church thrust above the trees. *Photograph by Alan Nyiri, 1991*

Rt. Reverend Thomas Galberry, O.S.A., D.D., was President of Villanova College from 1872 to 1876. It was under his presidency that the center and west wings of the College Building (Alumni Hall) were completed. Father Galberry was consecrated fourth Bishop of Hartford, Connecticut, on 19 March 1876. *Courtesy of Villanova University Archives*

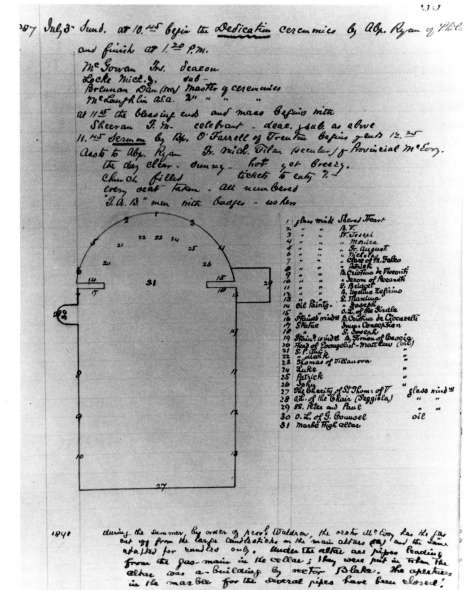

This page from Reverend Thomas C. Middleton's Journal shows the floor plan of the Saint Thomas of Villanova Church in 1887. *Courtesy of Augustinian Provincial Archives*

Reverend Joseph A. Coleman, O.S.A., was President of Villanova College from 1880 to 1886. Saint Thomas of Villanova Church was begun shortly after he succeeded to the presidency. *Courtesy of Villanova University Archives*

This view from the south shows Saint Thomas of Villanova Church and Augustinian Monastery (the former Belle-Air mansion after much renovation). (Lithograph by Packard, Butler and Partridge.) *Courtesy of Villanova University Archives*

Reverend Francis M. Sheeran, O.S.A., S.T.B., was President of Villanova College from 1886 to 1890. *Courtesy of Villanova University Archives*

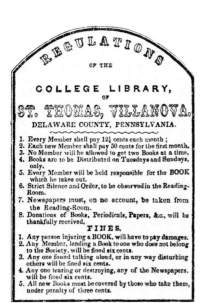

Regulations of the College Library when it was located on the second floor of the east wing of the College Building (Alumni Hall). The majority of the books in this library had been brought over from Europe by early Augustinians. *Courtesy of Villanova University Archives*

These students posed on the steps of the old College Building (now Alumni Hall). Composed of both college and academy boys, some members of the student body were as young as twelve. *Courtesy of Villanova University Archives*

This Villanova Baseball Team is from the late nineteenth century. On 2 May 1866, Villanova College's first varsity sport took the field when the baseball team played its very first game against the Central Club of Philadelphia. Villanova won, 74–9. *Courtesy of Villanova University Archives*

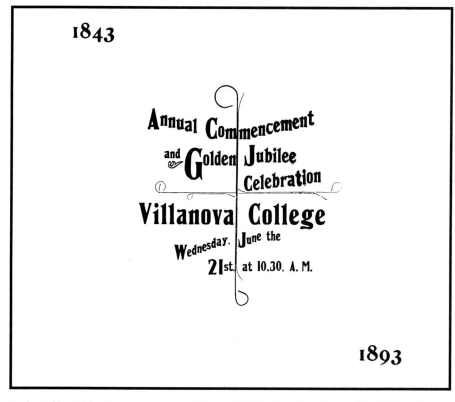

At the Golden Jubilee Commencement on 21 June 1893, His Grace Most Reverend Archbishop Patrick J. Ryan, D.D., of Philadelphia gave the address. *Courtesy of Villanova University Archives*

Reverend Christopher A. McEvoy, O.S.A., was President of Villanova College from 1890 to 1894. His term included the Golden Jubilee of 1893. *Courtesy of Villanova University Archives*

Reverend Thomas C. Middleton, O.S.A., D.D., was President of Villanova College from 1876 to 1878 and college librarian from 1865 to 1923. Middleton also organized and served as the first President of the American Catholic Historical Society of Philadelphia. *Courtesy of Villanova University Archives*

Historical Sketch of the Augustinian Monastery, College and Mission of St. Thomas of Villanova (1893), a fiftieth anniversary history of the college, was written by Reverend Thomas C. Middleton, O.S.A., D.D. *Courtesy of Villanova University Archives*

This bird's-eye view shows the Villanova campus from the north side, circa 1890. The front of the old College Building faces the tree-lined path which led to the train station and served as a gateway to campus. *Courtesy of Villanova University Archives*

Reverend John J. Fedigan, O.S.A., was President of
Villanova College from 1878 to 1880 and Augustinian
Provincial, Province of Saint Thomas of Villanova, from
1898 to 1902. This portrait by Thomas Eakins shows Father
Fedigan standing beside a drawing of new monastery
completed in 1901. (Oil on canvas.) *Courtesy of the
Augustinian Province of Saint Thomas of Villanova*

MONASTERY
OF
ST THOMAS
VILLA NOVA

CHAPTER TWO
Prosperity and Struggle, 1892–1942

Villanova's second half-century brought both expansion and decline. For several decades the college grew, propelled by a boom in the nation's economy, the increasing prosperity of local Catholics, and new academic programs. Buildings arose, intercollegiate athletics became a major force on campus, and student social life glittered with fancy balls and big-name bands. As the 1920s came to an end, Villanova could boast of a ten-fold increase in its student body in little more than three decades. Then the Great Depression struck, reducing student enrollment and forcing the college to postpone numerous building plans. The economy rebounded with World War II, but Villanova again faced the possibility of a smaller student population as hundreds of its young men joined the armed services.

A series of physical improvements at Villanova began shortly after the Golden Jubilee of 1892–1893. In the spring of 1895, for example, there was a new grandstand for the baseball diamond, located on the present Mendel Field. The same year the college built an iron archway over the path leading up from the railroad station, with the words VILLANOVA COLLEGE spelled out in gold letters. In 1896 the first electric lights appeared, and electric bells were installed in the president's and vice-president's offices, then located in the College Building (Alumni Hall). The following year asbestos coverings were applied to all the steam pipes, at a time when no one dreamed that asbestos posed a danger to health.

Reverend Francis J. McShane, O.S.A., was President of Villanova College from 1894 to 1895. *Courtesy of Villanova University Archives*

But it was in 1898 that the greatest physical changes began to take shape. In July, under the leadership of Reverend John J. Fedigan, O.S.A., Augustinian Provincial, the Provincial Chapter approved plans for a new monastery and Main College Hall (later Tolentine Hall). The two structures, rendered in gray stone and designed in the Collegiate Gothic style by Edwin F. Durang, would be built end to end and extend for some five hundred feet along the crest of a ridge facing the Lancaster Pike. Not everyone was happy about

Tolentine Hall, originally called College Hall and later Mendel Hall. This building was the administrative, academic, and residence center of the campus for many years. It was seriously damaged by fire on 28 January 1928 and rebuilt within its original walls in 1929. The hall was named in honor of Saint Nicholas of Tolentine in 1960. *Photograph by Peter Finger, 1992*

the decision, including three members of the college's Board of Trustees. Among them was Father Thomas C. Middleton, who believed that the project was far too expensive and joined others in denouncing it as "Fedigan's Folly." In truth, the total cost of $285,000, a tremendous sum in the 1890s, would prove a heavy burden for Villanova in the years just ahead.

Ground was broken for the monastery in March 1899 and for Main College Hall in November. The new Saint Thomas of Villanova Monastery opened in June 1901. Main College Hall was ready for occupancy in September of that year, al-

though the work was not entirely finished until 1902. For the first time the college students were separated physically from the academy boys, who remained at the old College Building (Alumni Hall). In their new headquarters the collegians enjoyed a gymnasium, dining room, and auditorium, in addition to a library, lecture halls, and modern laboratories. The building also contained administrative offices for the college. North of the new building lay the old athletic field (known to later generations as Mendel Field), which was much improved and included a new running track.

This construction required the demolition of two buildings. In April 1899, the former gymnasium and church, which had been built in 1869, fell to the wrecking crew. In August of 1902, the 1844 Chapel suffered the same fate.

This iron archway lead to campus with the words VILLANOVA COLLEGE spelled out in gold letters. A similar gate stood at the entrance to the Villanova train station. *Courtesy of Villanova University Archives*

This panorama shows Main College Hall, Augustinian Monastery, and Saint Thomas of Villanova Church in the early twentieth century. *Courtesy of Villanova University Archives*

The Belle-Air mansion remained, although renovations and additions had made the original house almost unrecognizable. No longer needed as a monastery, it was opened as a novitiate for the Augustinian community in December 1902. It was briefly known as Belle-Air Hall, but early in 1903 the name was changed to Saint Rita's. A fire on 10 January 1912 badly damaged the building. Its charred remains, which included the original Belle-Air mansion, were pulled down and replaced the same year by a new Saint Rita's Hall. It was designed in a simple Colonial Revival style, an architectural motif that was very popular throughout the country at that time, but one which did not blend well with the series of Gothic Revival structures that the college had begun with the Saint Thomas of Villanova Church in 1883. Yet its clean lines echoed the classical style of the College Building (Alumni Hall) which stood behind it. Saint Rita's classical dome likewise complemented the gilded dome atop the College Building.

The same year that Saint Rita's went up (1912) ground was broken for a new seminary building. Named for its donor, Bernard Corr, the structure was designed by Durang. Like the church that he had executed for the college in 1883, Corr was Gothic in design and thus fit well with the growing number of Gothic structures on

This is the gymnasium in Main College Hall in the early twentieth century. *Courtesy of Villanova University Archives*

Commencement in 1900 included the Laying of the Corner Stone for New College (Main College Hall). This building was called Mendel Hall from 1929 to 1960, and later Tolentine Hall. *Courtesy of Villanova University Archives*

campus. This Collegiate Gothic style was then favored on many campuses and was thought to give them a look of ancient respectability, the obvious model being the medieval universities of Europe and England.

The ambitious building campaign at the beginning of the twentieth century had been calculated to attract more students through improved facilities. At first the plan seemed to work. In 1901, the year that Main College Hall opened, total enrollment at Villanova (including the college, seminarians, and academy boys) increased to 124, 26 more than the year before. Enrollment reached 134 in 1902, but it dropped slightly to 132 by 1904.

One of the problems was Villanova's traditional curriculum, which remained grounded in ancient languages, mathematics, and philosophy. To many students and their parents such studies appeared impractical in a modern, industrial nation like the United States. During the latter third of the nineteenth century more and more colleges and universities accordingly had begun programs in science and engineering. In the fall of 1905 Villanova followed suit by launching an engineering school. That September total enrollment at Villanova jumped to 187 students and by the fall of 1915 it was close to 400, the same year that the college inaugurated a School of Science and a premedical course. The new programs, it seemed, were having a salutary effect.

The dining room in Main College Hall is seen here between 1902 and 1910. *Courtesy of Villanova University Archives*

The appearance of important individuals on the campus also heightened Villanova's public image. The commencement speaker for 1902 was former Presi-

34

dent of the United States Grover Cleveland, and in 1910 President William Howard Taft addressed the Villanova graduates. The Commencement speaker in 1918, when Villanova celebrated its seventy-fifth anniversary (or Diamond Jubilee) was Vice-President of the United States Thomas R. Marshall. All three speakers received honorary doctorates from Villanova.

By the time Vice-President Marshall visited the campus the United States had been officially involved in World War I for more than a year. Within two weeks of the American declaration in April 1917 Villanova students were forced to drill on the athletic field under military direction. A year later more than two hundred Villanova men were in the armed forces. In September 1918 a Student Army Training Corps (S.A.T.C.) began to train Army officers at Villanova. There were 274 men in the corps when it opened that fall. Most of them lived in Main College Hall, where a half dozen or more men were crammed into rooms designed for one or two persons.

At the end of September the deadly influenza epidemic struck the campus, and infected 173 students altogether. On 1 October the Army imposed a quarantine at Villanova, complete with guard posts at all the entrances. Seven nurses from the Bryn Mawr Hospital, aided by six Sisters of Saint Joseph, came to nurse the sick. Three Villanova students died before the epidemic lifted in November.

When news of the Armistice reached campus on 11 November 1918 three companies from the S.A.T.C. unit paraded through Bryn Mawr, where Reverend James Dean, O.S.A., the college President, was one of the speakers at a local ceremony. Afterwards the men marched back to campus where they lighted a huge

Old Mendel Field is seen here with the train station in the foreground. *Courtesy of Villanova University Archives*

Reverend Lawrence A. Delurey, O.S.A., D.D., was President of Villanova College from 1895 to 1910. *Courtesy of Villanova University Archives*

The much enlarged Belle-Air mansion of John Rudolph, purchased by the Augustinians in 1841, served as a monastery, residence hall, classroom building, and finally as a seminary building. It was named Saint Rita's Hall in early 1903 after the completion of a new monastery. *Courtesy of Villanova University Archives*

This is how Saint Rita's Hall appeared following the fire of 10 January 1912. These charred remains were taken down and replaced by the present Saint Rita's Hall (1912), which also functioned as a seminary building for several decades. The financial loss from the fire was put at $100,000. *Courtesy of Villanova University Archives*

This original lock and key from Belle-Air, the Rudolph mansion, is all that remains from the earliest college building. *Courtesy of Villanova University Archives*

bonfire and burned the German Kaiser in effigy.

The summer before the war ended Villanova started its first summer school program, created largely for the benefit of Roman Catholic nuns in the area. Several lay women and "college boys" also attended the first summer school in 1918. Ten years later, in 1928, the college initiated a Night School to which both men and women were admitted. At first, classes were held on the Villanova campus but in the mid-1930s they moved to Catholic high schools in Philadelphia in order to serve a wider audience. Although it may not have been evident at the time, the summer program and evening school were the first steps in a long evolution toward coeducation at Villanova.

It was just after World War I that Villanova opened a School of Commerce and Finance. The college had offered commercial courses for a number of years, but in 1921 it created a separate school, with degrees in appropriate subjects. By the end of the decade Commerce and Finance was the largest division on campus. Villanova also inaugurated a separate Graduate School in 1931. It appears that there had been graduate studies as early as 1911, but there was no organized division for another two decades. Through its graduate program Villanova offered master's degrees in several subjects. Two years later, in 1933, the college began a Department of Nursing, which twenty years later would become a separate undergraduate school.

The practicality of many of these new offerings, in addition to the economic boom of the 1920s, swelled enrollments to unanticipated levels. From approximately three hundred students at the beginning of the 1920s, enrollment reached a little more than one thousand in the early 1930s.

In order to provide facilities for its growing numbers, Villanova erected a series of new buildings. In fact, physical improvements began even before the great student expansion was evident. With funds raised by the alumni just after World War I, the venerable old College Building received a coat of stucco and a remodeled front entrance. A

Saint Rita's Hall built in 1912 to replace the burnt Belle-Air mansion, was designed by George F. Dobbin. It served as a seminary building for many years. *Courtesy of Villanova University Archives*

new gymnasium appeared on the ground floor of the east wing, where the Dramatic Hall had been located, and before that a study hall. In honor of the fund-raising efforts of its graduates, the structure was renamed Alumni Hall in October 1920.

In 1923 the preparatory school, by then known as Saint Nicholas of Tolentine Academy, moved off campus forever and relocated several miles away under the name of Malvern Prep. For those who had come to believe that the reputation of Villanova College was compromised by the existence of an academy on its grounds, the move to Malvern was a great relief.

It was also in 1923 that Villanova broke ground for Austin Hall, rendered in gray stone and designed in the Collegiate Gothic style as a dormitory for upper classmen. Opening in the fall of 1924, it contained a new college library in its east wing. The following year Villanova erected a small radio building (located on the present site of Vasey Hall and now demolished), which housed the college's first radio station. In 1928 authorities launched yet another dormitory for upper classmen. Named Fedigan Hall and completed in 1929, it resembled a stark Florentine palazzo

Reverend Edward G. Dohan, O.S.A., LL.D., was President of Villanova College from 1910 to 1917. *Courtesy of Villanova University Archives*

Corr Hall, completed in 1914, was designed by architect Edwin F. Durang, who had designed Saint Thomas of Villanova Church three decades before. Corr Hall served as the principal building for the Augustinian Seminary until 1964. *Courtesy of Villanova University Archives*

of the late Middle Ages. At the same time Villanova built an impressive football stadium along Lancaster Pike. The south stands were completed in 1927 and the north stands two years later.

As the 1920s came to an end college authorities supposed that the surging enrollments of the past decade would continue into the foreseeable future. Thus in January 1930 they announced an ambitious campaign to raise $2,300,000. The funds would be used for several projects. One was a cluster of five buildings, facing Lancaster Pike, on the East Campus. At the head of a new quadrangle was to be a Commerce and Finance building, to its right a free standing library building, and to its left a new dining hall. Also included in the projections were several dormitories and a large field house. Another $800,000 of the fund would be set aside as a permanent endowment, the first in Villanova's history. In addition to these plans for physical growth, the administration wished to slow the increase in enrollments, proposing to

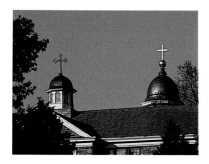

The domes and crosses of Alumni Hall (left) and Saint Rita's Hall are lifted high over the campus. *Photograph by Alan Nyiri, 1991*

Our Mother of Good Counsel Shrine evokes a feeling of peace and repose upon all who pass beneath her tranquil gaze. This seven-foot statue of white Carrara marble was designed by Daprato Studio, Pietrsanta, Italy. The shrine was erected by Dominic Cannito in 1954. Corr Hall is in the background. *Photograph by Alan Nyiri, 1992*

concentrate on higher admissions standards rather than on mere numbers. According to this scheme, the increases of the 1930s would be smaller than those of the twenties, with no more than two thousand students by 1940.

Despite the stock market crash in October 1929, no one at Villanova or anywhere else in the country realized that ten years of depression lay ahead. The college thus managed to erect the Commerce and Finance building, completed in 1931 (and soon thereafter called Vasey Hall). The next year Villanova completed the Field

House (later renamed Jake Nevin Field House) which featured a combined auditorium/gymnasium and swimming pool. But the tightening grip of the Great Depression stalled plans for the library, dormitories, and dining hall. The projected endowment also fell victim to the economic crisis. Student enrollment meanwhile began to plummet, and by 1935 it was down to seven hundred. Plans to raise admissions standards thus became impossible.

Just before the Great Depression Villanova suffered a second devastating fire, this time at Main College Hall. It was late on a Sunday afternoon, 28 January 1928, when students smelled smoke and began evacuating the building. Fire companies came from all over the area, but a heavy snow, which had been falling all day, kept several of them from reaching the scene. Morning revealed a blackened hulk, the insides of which had been completely destroyed. Immediately the college began rebuilding the interior, and by the fall of 1929 the building was ready for occupancy. The exterior looked much as it had

before, except for certain features on the upper story. The building was rechristened Mendel Hall, a label it would retain until 1960, when it was renamed Tolentine Hall and the name Mendel was given to a new science building.

The third great fire at Villanova swept through the Saint Thomas of Villanova Monastery on 2 August 1932. The building was so badly damaged that it had to be demolished. Despite the hard times, the Augustinian community managed to begin a new monastery in 1933. Completed a year later, it repeated the Gothic motifs of the earlier structure and was in many ways more attractive than the building it replaced.

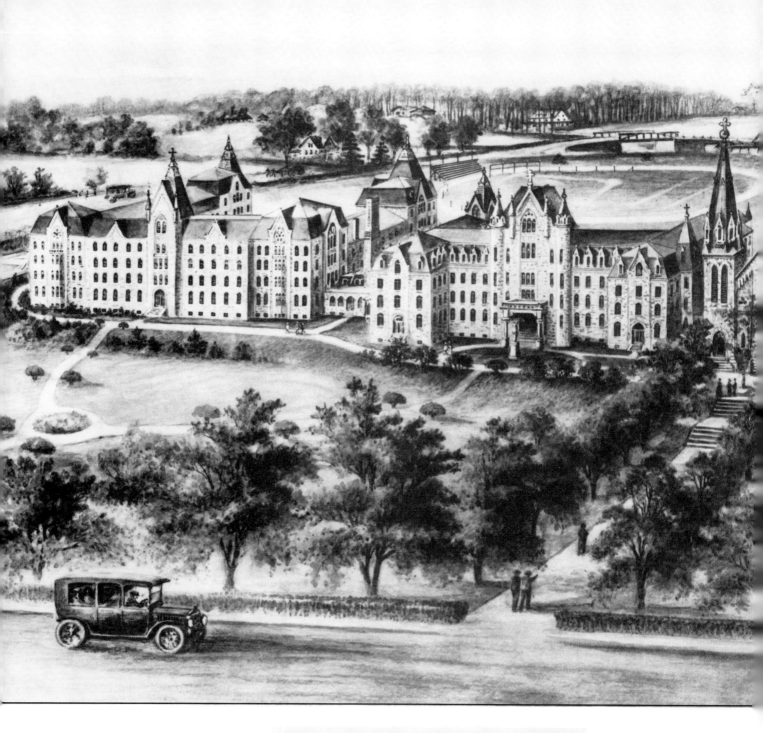

Ground Breaking for Corr Hall, the new Augustinian seminary, was on 4 May 1912. From left to right are Reverend Bernard J. O'Donnell, O.S.A.; Reverend Martin J. Geraghty, O.S.A., D.D., Augustinian Provincial; donor Bernard Corr; and Reverend Nicholas J. Vasey, O.S.A., S.T.L. *Courtesy of Villanova University Archives*

Villanova College, 1915. (Lithograph by E. A. Wright Bank Note Company, Philadelphia.) *Courtesy of Villanova University Archives*

During these early decades of the twentieth century student life at Villanova had undergone great change. The first student dance on campus would appear to be a Thanksgiving Dance, held in the gymnasium at Main College Hall on 28 November 1918 and sponsored by the S.A.T.C. The Villanova Jazz Band provided music for the evening. Beginning in 1920 many dances took place in the Alumni Hall gymnasium, while more elaborate balls migrated to one of the hotels in downtown Philadelphia. After the opening of the Field House in 1932 virtually all dances were held there. The most important of these was the Belle Air Ball, first hosted by the senior class in 1922, a winter social event that would endure at Villanova for more than four decades. Routine dances featured music by the Villanovans, a college dance band, while the more spectacular events demanded one of the big-name bands

Engineering students in the Machine Shop in the 1920s. *Courtesy of Villanova University Archives*

(Below) Students in the Physics Research Laboratory in the 1930s. The School of Science was established in 1915 to meet the growing demands for a specialized preparation for medical and dental schools. The four-year course led to a bachelor of science degree in biology. *Courtesy of Villanova University Archives*

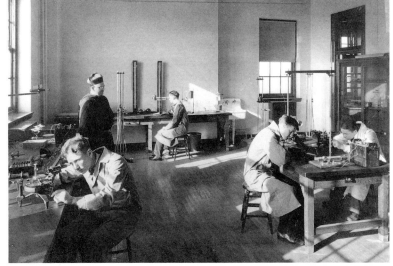

which flourished during this era. Among those who performed on campus were Ozzie Nelson (1933), Tommy and Jimmy Dorsey (1935), Isham Jones (1935), Glen Gray (1936), Jan Garber (1936), and Les Brown (1942).

Another long-lasting social tradition, known as Junior Week, began in 1924. It took place during the second week in May, when members of the junior class received their college blazers and walking canes for the first time. The week's events came to a climax with the annual Blazer Ball, to which juniors wore their blue blazers and white duck trousers in honor of the college colors of blue and white. In 1934 another Villanova tradition, Mother's Day, was added to Junior Week, as mothers were invited to visit the campus on the Monday after Mother's Day. This tradition would also last for several decades. Just as familiar as these events was the annual freshman hazing, which during the 1920s required initiation into the Eternal Order of Hobble Gobble. Freshmen also had to wear beanies and pay proper respect to upper classmen.

From the early 1920s the favorite student gathering place was the Pie Shop, operated by Louis ("Louie") Ciamaichela. Louie came to Villanova in 1922 as a barber and remained on campus for three decades, becoming a legend in his own lifetime to thousands of students. During this period the Pie Shop was in the basement of old Mendel Hall (the former Main College Hall and later Tolentine Hall).

Football also became a student preoccupation by the 1920s (Villanova's first football team having been organized in 1894). The most important game of the season was against Temple and was played in November. Students worked themselves up for the Temple game with a giant pep rally, followed by a huge bonfire. Football crowds were often so large during this period that some games had to be played in Philadelphia's Municipal Stadium. This was especially true in 1937 and

Former President of the United States Grover Cleveland was the Commencement speaker on 17 June 1902. He was granted an honorary doctor of jurisprudence, the first such degree given in the United States. *Courtesy of Villanova University Archives*

President of the United States William Howard Taft (left) gave the Commencement address on 18 June 1910 and received an honorary doctor of jurisprudence. In his address President Taft paid a high tribute to Pope Leo XIII, to the Roman Catholic church, and to its religious orders and their educational activities. Taft is accompanied by Reverend Lawrence A. Delurey, O.S.A., D.D., President of Villanova College from 1895 to 1910. *Courtesy of Public Relations*

(Below) A Student Army Training Corps (S.A.T.C.) began training Army officers at Villanova College in September 1918. This military unit was disbanded on 11 December 1918. *Courtesy of Villanova University Archives*

1938, when the Villanova eleven had two undefeated seasons in a row. It was in this epoch of football mania that all athletic teams at Villanova became known as the Wildcats. The name was suggested by assistant football coach Edward Hunsinger and was adopted by a vote of the student body in 1926.

Although the old Jug Books with their elaborate records of crime and punishment had long since disappeared, students still had to conform to a rigorous standard of behavior. For a time during the early decades of the twentieth century juniors and seniors wore academic gowns to all classes. During the 1920s and 1930s, they exchanged these for suits and ties. Students could not leave campus for any reason without signing out of the dormitory, and had to attend two religious retreats each year, in addition to religious services once a week.

In politics Villanova students preferred the Democratic party by a large margin, a position which reflected the fact that most Roman Catholics, particularly if they were of Irish descent, continued to favor the Democrats over the Republicans. Polls conducted by *The Villanovan*, the student newspaper, showed that students over-

Reverend James J. Dean, O.S.A., M.S., was President of Villanova College from 1917 to 1920. *Courtesy of Villanova University Archives*

Eighty-sixth Annual Commencement
Villanova College, Villanova, Penna., June 6th, 1929.

This family gathered around their graduate on graduation day, 8 June 1933. *Courtesy of Villanova University Archives*

(Top panorama) Nuns at Villanova Summer School. *Courtesy of Villanova University Archives*

(Bottom panorama) Villanova College Commencement of 6 June 1929. (Photograph by Harry D. Richards, Llanerch, Pennsylvania.) *Courtesy of Villanova University Archives*

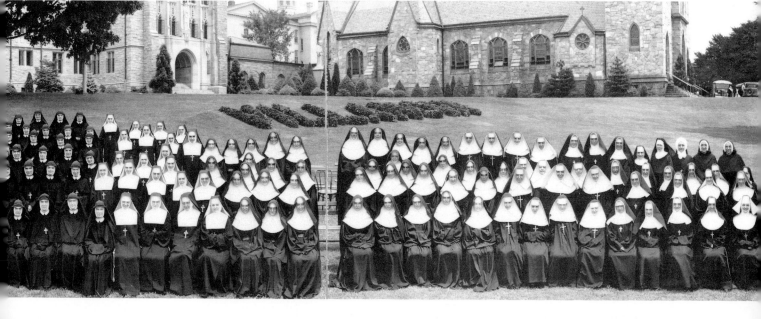

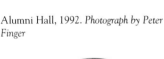

Alumni Hall, 1992. *Photograph by Peter Finger*

Reverend Francis A. Driscoll, O.S.A., LL.D., was President of Villanova College from 1920 to 1924. *Courtesy of Villanova University Archives*

The word *Academy*, chiseled and etched in gold above the front doorway of Alumni Hall, testifies to a time when few youngsters graduated from public schools. It also stands as a reminder that this building once housed both the Villanova College and Tolentine Academy. *Photograph by Peter Finger, 1992*

whelmingly supported Franklin D. Roosevelt in 1932 and again in 1936. In 1940, however, a small majority of students favored Wendell Willkie over Roosevelt, citing their opposition to a third term and also to Roosevelt's increasingly internationalist stance in foreign affairs.

Editorials and polls in *The Villanovan* showed that students as well as faculty were strongly isolationist during the 1930s and opposed American entry into World War II until the very eve of Pearl Harbor. The American declaration of war in early December 1941 put an end to this isolationism for the time being and Villanova was soon on a war footing for the second time in twenty-five years.

The war came just as the college was preparing to celebrate its one-hundredth anniversary in 1942–1943. The commemorations began on 20 September 1942 with a Solemn Pontifical Mass, celebrated by Dennis Cardinal Dougherty, Archbishop of Philadelphia. But the wartime emergency forced the college to curtail or cancel

The Alumni Banquet for the dedication of Alumni Hall was held in the new Alumni Hall gymnasium on 20 October 1920. *Courtesy of Villanova University Archives*

Austin Hall, a residence for upperclassmen was begun in 1923 and completed in 1924. It was the first of several new buildings at Villanova made necessary by the rapid growth of student enrollments in the 1920s. The building's design is attributed to Wilson Eyre, a highly respected Philadelphia architect. *Photograph by Alan Nyiri, 1991*

The third Villanova College Seal, adopted in 1911, restored the design of Villanova's first seal (1848). It features a Bible, cross, crozier, cincture, heart, and a motto of Saint Augustine's principles: *Veritas, Unitas, Caritas* ("Truth, Unity, and Charity"). This seal appears above the entrance to Austin Hall. *Photograph by Alan Nyiri, 1991*

most of the other activities which had been planned. Villanova thus entered its second century in an atmosphere of crisis and uncertainty.

The old Villanova College Library in the east wing of Austin Hall proved too small almost as soon as it was completed in 1924. Unfortunately, the Depression of the 1930s and then World War II forced the college to postpone the building of a new library for another two decades. *Courtesy of Villanova University Archives*

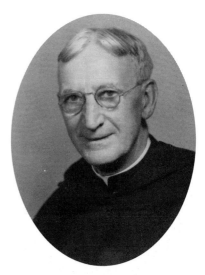

Reverend Joseph A. Hickey, O.S.A., D.D., was President of Villanova College from 1924 to 1925. *Courtesy of Villanova University Archives*

The Radio Building, 1925, served as a place for radio enthusiasts on campus. Later the commercialization of radio forced the station to shut down. It was razed to make room for the Commerce and Finance Building (Vasey Hall). During the emergency after the fire in 1928 it served as a makeshift dormitory. *Courtesy of Villanova University Archives*

Reverend Mortimer A. Sullivan, O.S.A., LL.D., was President of Villanova College from 1925 to 1926. *Courtesy of Villanova University Archives*

Villanova's Goodreau Stadium was built as part of a program of school expansion during the 1920s. The stadium honors Leo Francis Goodreau, who was fatally injured in a varsity football practice in 1928. The south side, seen here, was completed in 1927, but the construction of the north side was not finished until 1929. *Courtesy of Villanova University Archives*

The tribute given to Leo Francis Goodreau (1900–1928) by his affectionate classmates was: "Scholar, athlete, gentleman. To one who gave his life for Villanova College." *Courtesy of Villanova University Archives*

The projected quadrangle on East Campus, 1930, was designed by architect Paul Monaghan. *Courtesy of Villanova University Archives*

This scene followed the disastrous fire of 28 January 1928. At the time losses were estimated at two million dollars. Main College Hall was for many years the administrative, academic, and residential center of the campus. It was rebuilt in 1929 largely within the original exterior walls, and named in honor of Saint Nicholas of Tolentine in 1960. Between 1929 and 1960 it was known as Mendel Hall, which should not be confused with a later building of the same name. *Courtesy of Villanova University Archives*

Saint Thomas of Villanova Monastery was destroyed by the fire of 2 August 1932. *Courtesy of Villanova University Archives*

Reverend James H. Griffin, O.S.A., LL.D., was President of Villanova College from 1926 to 1932. *Courtesy of Villanova University Archives*

Lavish dances were held at the Field House for decades. This photograph was taken on 1 April 1932
at the formal opening of the Field House, designed by Paul Monaghan. *Courtesy of Villanova University Archives*

This 1927 college dance band, The Villanovans, made its first
appearance at Villanova in the fall of 1923. *Courtesy of Public Relations*

This play, *Look Who's Here*, was presented on 4 and 5 May 1933 by the Turf and Tinsel Club. The club put on annual comedies in which men took both male and female parts. *Courtesy of Villanova University Archives*

Villanova usually celebrated Mother's Day on the Monday after Mother's Day. This tradition began in 1934, and these mothers and sons participated in one of the early celebrations. This day also marked the beginning of Junior Week at Villanova, held during the second week of May. *Courtesy of Villanova University Archives*

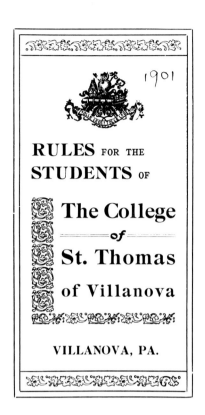

Courtesy of Villanova University Archives.

The Villanovan, first published in November 1916, then a monthly magazine. *Courtesy of Villanova University Archives*

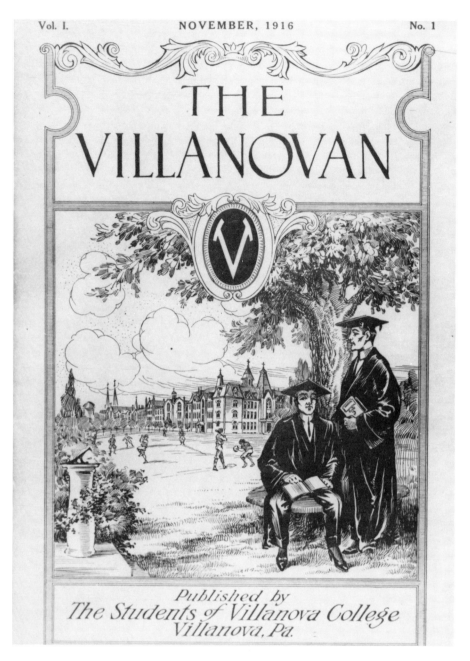

Vol. I.   NOVEMBER, 1916   No. 1

THE VILLANOVAN

Published by
The Students of Villanova College
Villanova, Pa.

A father helps his son move into Villanova College in 1933. *Courtesy of Villanova University Archives*

In the 1930s Railway Express Agency trucks delivered students' trunks. *Courtesy of Villanova University Archives*

Freshman initiation in 1939 for the Centennial Class of 1943 included this two-part freshman harmony, complete with ill-fitting clothes and silly gestures. Attentive sophomore "orienters" look on. *Courtesy of Villanova University Archives*

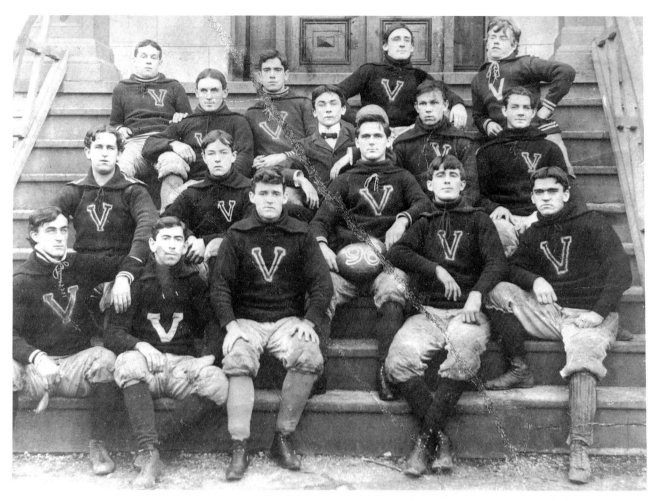

Villanova's football team played its first
game in 1894 against Logan A.A. at
Villanova which they won 24–0, under the
coaching of Michael J. Murphy. This is the
1896 team. *Courtesy of Villanova University
Archives*

Villanova's Cheerleaders prepare for the big game in front of the
Field House in 1937. *Courtesy of Villanova University Archives*

Clipper Smith and Harry Stuhldreher, circa 1925, were football
coaches at Villanova College in the 1920s.

Villanova Wildcat Football Coach Andy Talley and his staff began in 1984 to build up the team and the winning Wildcat spirit that characterizes Villanova athletics. *Photograph by Alan Nyiri, 1991*

The most popular member of any cheerleading squad is always the Wildcat. *Photograph by Alan Nyiri 1991.*

From freshmen orientation to graduation, the Villanova Band gives sound and color to the most important moments of a student's life. *Photograph by Alan Nyiri, 1991*

His Eminence Dennis Cardinal Dougherty, Archbishop of Philadelphia is seen here in procession of Solemn Pontifical Mass on 20 September 1942. *Courtesy of Villanova University Archives.*

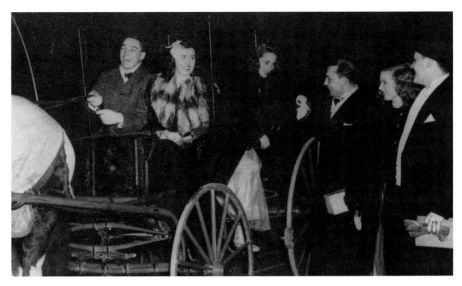

This horse and carriage was used to transport Centennial Ball guests to and from rail and bus stations on 15 January 1943. In addition to symbolizing Villanova's roots in the pre-automobile age, the horse and carriage were a practical response to gasoline rationing in 1943. *Courtesy of Villanova University Archives*

Solemn Pontifical Mass was celebrated by His Eminence Dennis Cardinal Dougherty, Archbishop of Philadelphia in the Villanova College Field House on 20 September 1942. The Most Reverend Gerald P. O'Hara preached the sermon. Three thousand celebrated the Augustinian institution's one hundredth anniversary. *Courtesy of Villanova University Archives*

This Centennial memorabilia features the Sister Liberty Bell, which once served as the Villanova College bell. Standing next to the bell is Reverend Joseph I. Boyle, O.S.A., M.A., chairman of the Villanova College Centennial celebration. *Courtesy of Villanova University Archives*

Students and faculty processing from Saint Thomas of Villanova Church to the Field House at Commencement in 1944. *Courtesy of Villanova University Archives*

For many years the Villanova Field House was the focus of Villanova athletics and student social events. When it first opened its doors the college's enrollment was approximately one thousand students. The field house was named in honor of trainer John "Jake" Nevin on 27 February 1985. *Photograph by Alan Nyiri, 1991*

Vasey Hall, built in 1930, was originally known as the Commerce and Finance Building. It was later named for the Augustinian Provincial Reverend Nicholas J. Vasey, O.S.A., S.T.L., from 1918 to 1926. Today it serves as an academic building and theatre, designed by architect Paul Monaghan. *Photograph by Alan Nyiri, 1991*

St. Thomas of Villanova Monastery was named in honor of Saint Thomas of Villanova, a sixteenth-century Augustinian archbishop and educator. This structure, designed by architects Henry D. Dagit and Sons, was built to replace the monastery of 1899 which was destroyed by fire on 2 August 1932. The dome of Alumni Hall is visible on the right. *Photograph by Alan Nyiri, 1991*

This fourth college seal was designed for Villanova's Centennial by Reverend John J. Vranna, O.S.A., M.A. The Board of Trustees approved it on 24 March 1942. *Courtesy of Villanova University Archives*

This grotto at Villanova College once stood near the Falvey Memorial Library. *Courtesy of Villanova University Archives*

CHAPTER THREE
College to University, 1942–1967

The twenty-five years following Villanova's Centennial began amidst war and uncertainty, and ended in an era of rapid growth and structural change. First the veterans of World War II and then the baby boom generation flooded the campus with thousands of students. Facilities were strained to the limit, forcing Villanova to purchase or erect almost two dozen buildings. New academic programs emerged, the administration reorganized itself, and Villanova became a university in name as well as in fact. Many well-known speakers visited the campus during this period, as did famous musicians and symphony orchestras. The number of women on campus also increased, yet in some ways student life changed very little from the prewar period.

Army Enlisted Reserve students have their last dinner at Villanova on 4 April 1943 before reporting for active duty. *Courtesy of Villanova University Archives*

The American declaration of war in late 1941 posed a serious threat to Villanova, which had just begun to recover from the Great Depression. It was evident that the war effort would last for several years and require millions of young men to serve in the armed forces. For an all-male institution like Villanova this was a potential disaster, as every able-bodied student would be expected to serve his country. The loss of students was not so great as anticipated in 1942–1943, since the military did not have sufficient training facilities to handle large numbers of men.

In fact, military authorities allowed college students to join the Army Enlisted Reserve program and remain in school until they were called into active service, at which time they would be evaluated further for officers training. The Villanova reserve unit received its call for 5 April 1943. The men had a special dinner at the college the night before and left by train early the next morning. Faculty and students walked down to the Villanova station with the men to wave a last good-bye.

Villanova was saved from a more drastic decline in enrollment by the Navy V-12 Program, which the college's President, Reverend Edward V. Stanford, O.S.A., had helped to establish as a member of the Secretary of the Navy's Civilian Advisory Committee. The twelve programs, established on college and university campuses throughout the United States, were created to train Naval officers. On 1 July 1943 some 600 V-12 recruits descended on Villanova College, where they were outfitted at the Field House. The V-12 students lived in the college dormitories and attended both regular and special classes in the college buildings.

Doctor Harold F. Hartmann says good-bye at the Villanova train station to an Army Enlisted Reserve student just before his departure for duty on 5 April 1943. *Courtesy of Villanova University Archives*

(Opposite page) This photograph shows Villanova NROTC midshipmen on parade during an alumni Homecoming football game. Although a World War II Navy V-12 unit was formed in 1943, it was not until three years later that the Naval ROTC was officially established. *Courtesy of Public Relations*

Reverend Edward V. Stanford, O.S.A., LL.D., was President of Villanova College from 1932 to 1944. *Courtesy of Villanova University Archives*

In order to accommodate them, as well as others who required an accelerated schedule, Villanova adopted a wartime calendar which featured three full semesters and three graduations each year. As in World War I, there was a Victory Garden on the slope between Corr Hall and the railroad tracks. The war also brought more women to campus during the summer, as they joined civilian men in taking technical classes which prepared them to work in war industries.

Villanova students learned of Japan's surrender on 14 August 1945 from the ringing of the college bell. Many entered the chapel to give thanks and then spilled out onto Austin Field where the band congregated for an impromptu parade. A local fire truck showed up and added its clanging bell to the celebrations. At least sixty-five Villanovans had given their lives to make this victory possible.

Few, if any, anticipated what the return of peace would mean to the one-hundred-year-old college. Just before the American entry into the war, Villanova's enrollment had almost rebounded to its pre-Depression levels and stood at approxi-

Navy V-12 recruits were outfitted at Villanova Field House on 1 July 1943. That fall the naval trainees made up approximately three-fourths of the student body. Without them, the campus would have been nearly deserted. *Courtesy of Villanova University Archives*

(Below) Navy V-12 students, 24 July 1943. *Courtesy of Villanova University Archives*

These Navy V-12 students are shown walking away from the old Commerce and Finance Building (the present Vasey Hall). *Courtesy of Augustinian Provincial Archives*

Father Stanford's identification badge. *Courtesy of Villanova University Archives*

Because of huge postwar enrollments and a subsequent shortage of rooms, Villanova converted the Field House into a temporary residence hall as seen here in 1947. *Courtesy of Villanova University Archives*

mately one thousand. Now that the war was over and the former servicemen were eligible for free tuition and fees and a modest living allowance though the G.I. Bill of Rights, hundreds of thousands of veterans showed up at colleges and universities all over the country. Some two thousand students arrived at Villanova in the fall of 1946, almost twice the pre-war high, forcing the college to set up rows of bunk beds on the Field House floor in order to accommodate them. The next year Villanova acquired several old Army barracks which it erected

These old Army barracks, known as Vets Village, were erected on the East campus as temporary structures to accommodate the large increase in students after World War II. *Courtesy of Villanova University Archives*

on the East Campus. These contained dormitories, classrooms, offices, and a new Pie Shop, presided over by the redoubtable "Louie."

The college also began a series of permanent buildings. These postwar constructions were arranged in two groups, with one cluster bordering Mendel Field on the

These students lived in some of the barracks on East Campus, circa 1950. *Courtesy of Villanova University Archives*

"Louie" (Louis Ciamaichela) managed the Villanova "Pie Shop," a campus snack bar and short order restaurant, for several decades. He was very popular with the students and became a living legend. *Courtesy of Villanova University Archives*

west side of campus, and another on the east side. The Mendel Field group included a library (now Falvey Hall), begun in 1947. Built of gray stone and exhibiting many features of the modernist (or International) style, it also contained pointed openings which echoed the Gothic forms of its older neighbors across the field. Two other buildings begun in 1947 were placed along the northern edge of Mendel Field. These were the Chemical Engineering building and a Navy ROTC building. The latter housed a permanent officers training program for the Navy, which replaced the V-12 program just after the war.

The Reference Room in Falvey Hall, seen here on 29 October 1964, was used by students from 1949 until 1967 when the library moved to its present location. *Courtesy of Villanova University Archives*

Reverend Francis X. N. McGuire, O.S.A., D.D., was President of Villanova College and University from 1944 to 1954. *Courtesy of Villanova University Archives*

The last of this group was a new science building called Mendel Hall (1960). Old Mendel Hall (alias Main College Hall) was renamed Tolentine Hall, a switch which caused much confusion at the time, and which will plague historians of Villanova so long as both buildings continue to stand. Like the library, the Chemical Engineering, the NROTC building, and the new Mendel Hall were all executed in gray stone, but their references to the Gothic style were confined to the doorways and were barely recognizable.

In the mid-1950s Villanova finally began to develop a quadrangle on the East Campus, an idea which had been proposed twenty-five years earlier. There it erected twin dormitories: Sullivan Hall (1954) on the north side of the quadrangle and Sheehan Hall (1957) on the south side. At the east end of this configuration stood a new Commerce and Finance building (1956), which was later named Bartley Hall. Faced in the now familiar gray stone, the three new buildings included the same sparse references to the Gothic style as the new structures around Mendel Field.

In the very center of the campus, the college began a new student center in 1954. Named Dougherty Hall, it contained a new Pie Shop (apparently without the legendary "Louie"), a student dining room, pool tables, a barber shop, radio station,

Aerial view of campus, early 1950s. *Courtesy of Villanova University Archives*

Chemicals in a science laboratory in Mendel Hall silhouetted against the soaring twin spires of Saint Thomas of Villanova Church. They symbolize the two-fold traditions of faith and learning at Villanova. *Photograph by Alan Nyiri, 1991*

Symbols of biology, chemistry, mathematics, astronomy, and physics appear on Mendel Hall above the main entrance. This hall was named in honor of the Augustinian monk Gregor J. Mendel, the father of modern genetics. *Photograph by Peter Finger, 1992*

The Mendel Medal, featuring the image of Augustinian Monk Gregor Mendel, was established by Villanova College in 1928. The medal is awarded to outstanding scientists. *Courtesy of Public Relations*

and offices for student organizations. Its pointed cupola added an attractive feature to Villanova's already impressive skyline of crosses, domes, and spires.

The last major building of the period was Saint Mary's Hall (1962), a large complex across Spring Mill Road, which was put up by the Augustinians to house a growing seminary. As a seminary building its features were more obviously Gothic than the other postwar structures. In addition to these major projects, Villanova purchased a number of residences which bordered the campus. Some of these became small dormitories, while others provided much needed office space.

By the time that Saint Mary's was completed in 1964 total enrollment at Villanova was approximately seventy-five hundred students. Contributing to these numbers were two new programs, a College of Nursing, formally opened in 1953 and the Villanova School of Law, which was established the same year. Villanova had offered courses in nursing for twenty years, but they were not given on campus and they did not lead to the bachelor's degree. Now there would be a full-fledged degree program on campus. The nurses occupied Austin Hall in the early years, placing the young women right in the center of campus.

Thanks to a large bequest, the law school began its own facility, Garey Hall, in 1956. Located between the railroad tracks and Spring Mill Road, Garey Hall's stone walls, Gothic entrance, and central spire blended well with other recent buildings.

Besides these major additions to the physical plant, Villanova reintroduced courses in radio, along with a new radio station, in 1947. In 1954 it offered a course in television. Villanova established an Honors Program in 1959, which, over the years would do much to strengthen the curriculum. At the same time enrollment in the Division of Liberal Arts and Sciences began to catch up with and then surpass the Commerce and Finance School. Commerce and Finance grew tremendously right after the war and remained the largest division on campus until 1962, when its standards were tightened and enrollments began to stabilize. Thereafter, Liberal Arts and Sciences was the largest division on campus.

With two professional schools (Law and Nursing), various graduate programs, an engineering school, and wide offerings in the arts, sciences, and business, Villanova had become a university. In order to make this fact official, Villanova secured a special act from the Pennsylvania state legislature. The bill was signed by the governor on 26 August 1953, and on 18 November 1953 the Court of Common Pleas of Delaware County approved the official change from the "Augustinian College of Villanova" to "Villanova University in the State of Pennsylvania."

Within several years it became clear that Villanova's administrative structure would have to change in order to accommodate its greater complexity and university status. In 1956 it created three vice-presidents, one each for Academic Affairs,

In the Mendel Hall Observatory from left to right are Doctor Sallie L. Baliunas, a researcher at the Harvard Smithsonian Center for Astrophysics; the Reverend Edward F. Jenkins, O.S.A., Ph.D., founder of the Villanova Astronomy Department; Daniel Zirpoli, director of the Davis Planetarium in the Maryland Science Center; and Dr. Edward F. Guinan, Jr., member of the Villanova Astronomy Department and a nationally recognized astronomer and researcher. *Courtesy of Villanova University Archives*

Students listen to music and converse in Sullivan Hall, 1959. This residence hall was named for Reverend Mortimer A. Sullivan, O.S.A., LL.D., who was President of Villanova from 1925 to 1926 and Augustinian Provincial from 1932 to 1938 and 1944 to 1949. *Courtesy of Villanova University Archives*

Sheehan Hall, built in 1957, was named in honor of Reverend John T. Sheehan, O.S.A., J.C.D., Augustinian Provincial from 1938 to 1944. This residence hall was designed by architects Henry D. Dagit and Sons. *Photograph by Alan Nyiri, 1991*

This academic building, designed by architects Henry D. Dagit and Sons, was named for Reverend Joseph C. Bartley, O.S.A., Ph.D., Dean of the College of Commerce and Finance from 1921 to 1962. *Photograph by Peter Finger, 1992*

A Barber Shop was located in one of the barracks erected after World War II. It moved to the new Dougherty Hall, circa 1955. *Courtesy of Villanova University Archives*

Financial Affairs, and Student Affairs. In 1961 it added a vice-president for Public Relations and Development. The following year (1962) the various academic divisions were renamed colleges, and their deans were given authority commensurate with their positions.

Although there were many more students at Villanova than there were in the past, student life did not change dramatically after World War II. The major social events survived into the postwar period, including Mother's Day, Junior Week, the Belle Air Ball, and other dances. The same kinds of big bands which had provided music in the past continued to come after the war. In 1957 Guy Lombardo and his orchestra played for the Senior Prom. Two years later the seniors chose the Glen Miller orchestra, under the direction of Ray McKinley. If anything, the decorations were even more impressive than in the past, attesting to the seriousness with which students regarded their dances. In 1951 the juniors adopted a Parisian theme for their prom, complete with a thirty-foot model of the Eiffel Tower rising from the Field House floor. The following year the seniors chose the popular musical, *On the Town*, for their theme and constructed an eighty-foot model of the Brooklyn Bridge as the centerpiece of their decorations.

It was the following year, in 1953, that a new social event began at Villanova, the annual Shamokinaki Dance, held to aid Augustinian missionaries in Japan. The name derived from the hometown of Reverend Thomas P. Purcell, O.S.A., one of the missionaries, who was from Shamokin, Pennsylvania. The "aki" was added to

The spire of Dougherty Hall is viewed through colorful foliage. This building was named for Reverend Joseph M. Dougherty, O.S.A., Ph.D., Augustinian Provincial from 1950 to 1954, and longtime professor. Designed by architects Henry D. Dagit and Sons, it once served as the Villanova Student Center. *Photograph by Peter Finger, 1991*

The Fourth Centennial celebration of Saint Thomas of Villanova was on 22 September 1955. Left to right: Reverend Henry E. Greenlee, O.S.A., S.T.D., Augustinian Provincial, Saint Thomas of Villanova Province; Reverend James A. Donnellon, O.S.A., Ph.D., President; His Eminence Francis Cardinal Spellman, D.D., Archbishop of New York who received a honorary doctor of literature; and His Excellency the Most Reverend John Francis O'Hara, C.S.C., D.D., Archbishop of Philadelphia. *Courtesy of Villanova University Archives*

give it a Japanese flavor. Pagodas, archways, and lanterns lent an Oriental theme to the dance, held each year in the Field House. Another charitable event, begun in 1948, was the annual Christmas party which Villanova students held for the children of Saint John's Orphanage in Philadelphia.

Although the social events of the postwar period were similar to those of earlier years, a new note of informality was evident in many of them. There had been a number of informal dances during the war and these continued into peacetime. In 1949, for example, the juniors voted to hold an informal Blazer Ball, which meant that juniors did not have to wear their blazers to the affair. Many other dances replaced formal attire with a conventional suit and tie. Yearbook photographs also reveal that some men were no longer wearing ties to class by the early 1950s. Then in the 1960s concerts by popular singing groups began to vie in student popularity with the traditional round of dances. In 1956 Villanova hosted the Four Aces; in

The "Pie Shop" in Dougherty Hall, 1955. *Courtesy of Villanova University Archives*

1965, Peter, Paul, and Mary; and in 1967, Simon and Garfunkle.

Balancing purely social events were a variety of speakers and serious musical performances. Several renowned symphony orchestras visited the campus: Leopold Stokowski and the American Symphony Orchestra (1963); George Szell and the Cleveland Orchestra (1966); Leonard Bernstein and the New York Philharmonic (1966); Eugene Ormandy and the Philadelphia Orchestra (1967); Wolfgang Sawallisch and the Vienna Orchestra (1967). Popular performers also came to Villanova. Louis "Satchmo" Armstrong played at the Field House in early 1958, and beginning in 1961 Villanova hosted an intercollegiate jazz festival. Famous jazz bands highlighted this event, as in 1965 when Stan Kenton made an appearance.

The list of noted speakers on campus during this period is long and impressive. Among them were Senator Edmund Muskie (1959); Chicago Mayor Richard Daley (1964); philosopher and educator Mortimer Adler (1964); U.S. Supreme Court Justice Arthur Goldberg (1965); social critic Vance Packard (1966); consumer advocate Ralph Nader (1966); and poet W. H. Auden (1967). On 27 April 1957 John F. Kennedy, United States Senator from Massachusetts and future President of the United States, was present for the dedication of the Law School building (Garey Hall). Reverend Doctor Martin Luther King, Jr., gave an address in the Field House on 20 January 1965.

During the 1950s and 1960s many campus speakers addressed themselves to the dangers of Communism, including former Communist Elizabeth Bentley (1951),

Students dining room in Dougherty Hall, 1955. *Courtesy of Villanova University Archives*

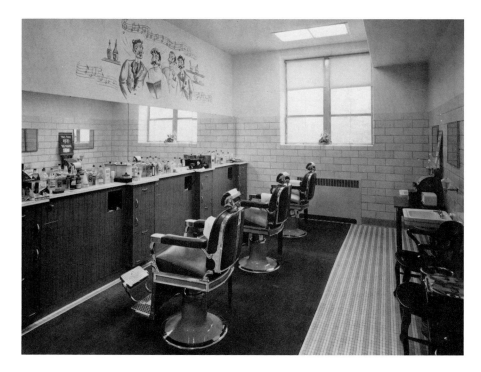

Barber Shop in Dougherty Hall, 1955.
Courtesy of Villanova University Archives

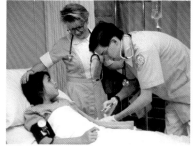

These 1992 Villanova undergraduate nursing students in uniform are administering medication to a patient under supervision. The nursing program opened full-time undergraduate study to women for the first time. *Photograph by Alan Nyiri, 1992*

U.S. Senator Thomas Dodd (1961), and Villanova's own Reverend Charles J. McFadden, O.S.A. (1962), a leading writer on the philosophy of Communism. *The Villanovan* also carried scores of editorials on the Communist threat during the postwar period.

For a variety of reasons Villanova students continued to favor the Democrats in presidential elections. *The Villanovan* did not conduct a poll in 1944 because of the war, but in 1948 students chose Democrat Harry S. Truman over Republican Thomas E. Dewey. In 1952 they selected Democrat Adlai Stevenson by a large majority in his race against Republican Dwight D. Eisenhower—this despite Eisenhower's immense popularity in the nation at large. The rematch between Stevenson and Eisenhower in 1956 found Villanovans preferring Eisenhower by a slim margin, but in 1960 Democrat John F. Kennedy was the overwhelming choice of students against Republican Richard M. Nixon, in part because Kennedy, if elected, would become the first Roman Catholic president in American history. Four years later, in 1964, students gave a huge vote to Democrat Lyndon B. Johnson who opposed Republican Barry Goldwater.

Villanova University observed its 125th anniversary in 1967–1968 with a num-

Saint Mary's Hall, built in 1962, housed the Augustinian Seminary at Villanova until 1972 and later served as a residence hall and the College of Nursing. It was designed by architects Henry D. Dagit and Sons. *Photograph by Peter Finger, 1991*

ber of events, including dinners, a concert at Philadelphia's Academy of Music, and a Pontifical Mass celebrated by John Cardinal Krol, Archbishop of Philadelphia. These observances took place as tensions were beginning to rise on campus. In the years just ahead student protests, along with a series of academic and social reforms, would transform Villanova in many ways.

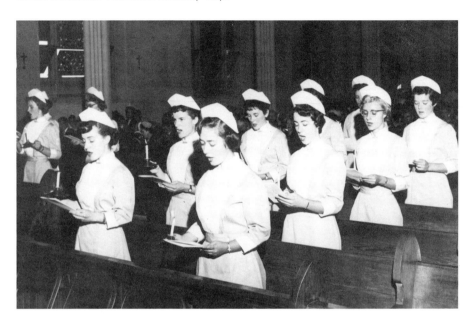

These sophomore nursing students had their Capping Ceremony in Saint Thomas of Villanova Church in 1959. Holding in their right hands the traditional candles, they recited the Villanova Nurses' Pledge: "I solemnly pledge myself before God . . . to pass my life in purity [,] . . . practice my profession faithfully [,] . . . and devote myself to the welfare of those committed to my care." These words of dedication marked the first milestone in their nursing careers. Villanova's first Capping exercise took place on 8 May 1955. Reverend James A. Donnellon, O.S.A., Ph.D., was President. *Courtesy of Villanova University Archives*

Basic nursing students at a Villanova wear a distinctive uniform. The Villanova "V" is incorporated into both the uniform and the cap, and the college's blue and white colors appear in both. These students received their caps on 12 February 1956. *Courtesy of Villanova University Archives*

Garey Hall houses the Villanova University School of Law. It was named for Eugene Lester Garey, (1891–1953), an eminent lawyer and benefactor. The 1956 building, seen here in 1970, was designed by architects Henry D. Dagit and Sons. *Courtesy of Villanova University Archives*

The Honorable John F. Kennedy, then U.S. Senator from Massachusetts, received an honorary doctor of laws degree during the Convocation at the Dedication of the Villanova Law School on 27 April 1957. Left to right are Reverend James A. Donnellon, O.S.A., Ph.D., President of Villanova University; Future U.S. President Kennedy; and the Honorable Richardson Dilworth, Mayor of Philadelphia. *Courtesy of Villanova University Archives.*

Reverend James A. Donnellon, O.S.A., Ph.D., was President of Villanova University from 1954 to 1959. *Courtesy of Villanova University Archives*

IN THE COURT OF COMMON PLEAS
OF DELAWARE COUNTY, PENNSYLVANIA
VILLANOVA UNIVERSITY OF

NUMBER: 2332

THE STATE OF PENNSYLVANIA JUNE TERM 1953

DECREE

AND NOW, this 18th day of November, A.D. 1953, upon motion of Joseph P. Gaffney, Esquire, and Joseph T. Mullray, Esquire, attorneys for the Petitioner, an application having been made to the Court for the amendment of the Charter and the Articles of Amendment of "The Augustinian College of Villa Nova, in the State of Pennsylvania", and having been presented to the Court for approval, accompanied by proof of publication of the required notice and a certified copy of the resolution authorizing the amendment, the Court after examination of the said instruments does hereby certify the proposed amendment to be lawful and does not conflict with the Non-Profit Corporation Law, and that it will be beneficial and not injurious to the community. It is, therefore, ordered, adjudged and decreed that the Articles of Amendment of "The Augustinian College of Villa Nova, in the State of Pennsylvania" be and that the same are hereby approved and upon the recording of the said Articles of Amendment and this Decree, the amendment specified in the Articles of Amendment shall become part of the original Charter, and it is further Ordered, Adjudged and Decreed that the name of the Petitioner is hereby changed to:

VILLANOVA UNIVERSITY
IN THE STATE OF PENNSYLVANIA

BY THE COURT,

Harold L. Ervin
PRESIDENT JUDGE

Henry S. Avery
Wm. R. Toal
Arthur P. Bretherick
ASSOCIATE JUSTICES

This decree marked the beginning of Villanova's legal existence as a university on 18 November 1953. Depicted in the illuminated capital "A" are from left to right: Reverend Francis X. N. McGuire, O.S.A., D.D.; Reverend Joseph M. Dougherty, O.S.A., Ph.D.; and Reverend James A. Donnellon, O.S.A., Ph.D. *Courtesy of Reverend Edmund J. Dobbin, O.S.A., S.T.D., President of Villanova University*

Pennsylvania Governor John S. Fine signed House Bill 581 on 26 August 1953, which enabled Villanova to become a university. *Courtesy of Public Relations*

Reverend John A. Klekotka, O.S.A., D.Sc., was President of Villanova University from 1959 to 1965. *Courtesy of Villanova University Archives*

Campus Police, 1962. *Courtesy of Villanova University Archives.*

These students took their final exams *en masse* at Villanova field House in 1955. *Courtesy of Villanova University Archives*

The highlight of the Junior Prom in 1955 was the crowning of "Mickey" (Mary Inez) Connell as "Queen of Junior Week" by band leader Johnny Long. Her escort was Henry "Hank" Smith. *Courtesy of Villanova University Archives*

Varsity Club members tote a few "Johnnies" on their shoulders at the annual orphans' party held in December 1955. *Courtesy of Villanova University Archives*

(Below) After a long day the Augustinians gather in the Common Room of Saint Thomas of Villanova Monastery to enjoy such activities as billiards, watch a televised sport, or perhaps engage in table tennis as do these two masters of the game, Reverend Joseph G. Kemme, O.S.A., M.S., and Reverend John A. Klekotka, O.S.A., M.S., in 1948. *Courtesy of Villanova University Archives*

Singer, song writer, and musician Jim Croce, seen here in 1965, was a psychology major who became interested in music after entering Villanova. He died in a plane crash, along with the pilot and four members of his group, at Natchitoches, Louisiana, on 20 September 1973. James J. Croce was thirty at the time of his death. *Courtesy of Villanova University Archives*

Eugene Ormandy (right) and the Philadelphia Orchestra performed at Villanova on 20 September 1967. *Courtesy of Villanova University Archives*

David Rabe, renowned playwright, launched his career while a student and faculty member of Villanova's Department of Theatre. *Courtesy of Villanova University Archives*

Villanova students drive past a local Eisenhower campaign headquarters in 1956. *Courtesy of Villanova University Archives*

Reverend Doctor Martin Luther King, Jr., civil rights leader and Nobel Prize winner, gives an address at Villanova on 20 January 1965. He explains why every person must have something he is willing to die for. *Courtesy of Villanova University Archives*

Each year Villanova University commemorates the life and work of Martin Luther King, Jr., with a candlelight march and vigil on his birthday. *Photograph by Alan Nyiri, 1992*

The Seal of Villanova University can be seen in the foyer of Falvey Memorial Library.

Courtesy of Villanova University Archives.

Reverend Charles J. McFadden, O.S.A.,
Ph.D., was a recognized expert in the
subjects of Communism and Medical Ethics.
Courtesy of Public Relations

Christianity Confronts Communism

by
Charles J. McFadden, O.S.A.,
Ph.D.

Franciscan Herald Press
1434 W. 51st St.
Chicago, Ill. 60609

Reverend Charles J. McFadden, O.S.A., Ph.D., continued to write after retirement from teaching. In
1982 he published *Christianity Confronts Communism*, a basic handbook on Communism for general
readership. *Courtesy of Villanova University Archives*

Reverend Joseph A. Flaherty, O.S.A.,
Ph.D., President of Villanova University
from 1965 to 1967. *Courtesy of Villanova
University Archives*

Villanova University's 125th Anniversary Logo. *Courtesy of Villanova University Archives*

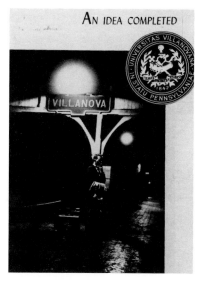

Villanova Student at Train Station, *The Belle Air*, 1954. An idea completed. The idea—"To open the mind, to correct it, to refine it, to enable it to know, and to digest, master, rule, and use its knowledge to give it power over its own facilities is an object of Liberal Education. It is a seat of wisdom, a light of the world, a minister of faith, an Alma Mater of the rising generation."— John Henry Newman, *The Idea of a University*.

Methodist Bishop Frederick Pierce Corson (left); His Eminence John Cardinal Krol, Archbishop of Philadelphia (center); and Reverend Robert J. Welsh, O.S.A., S.T.D., President of Villanova University (right) are on their way to the Pontifical Mass during the 125th anniversary celebration on 13 September 1967. *Courtesy of Villanova University Archives*

The presidential medallion is surrounded
by those of Villanova's colleges.

CHAPTER FOUR
Challenge and Renewal, 1967–1992

The past quarter-century of Villanova history has been marked by upheaval and resurgence. This period began with reforms in governance, the advent of complete coeducation, and student rebellion; it ended with wide recognition for Villanova's academic excellence and the celebration of the university's sesquicentennial year. Enrollment continued to grow, but not so rapidly as it did in the decades just before, as the baby boom came to an end and the university decided to consolidate its gains and to raise admission standards. The 1960s in particular turned out to be a watershed for Villanova, with many of the familiar rhythms of college life disappearing forever.

In 1968, just after completing its 125th anniversary, the university's Board of Trustees voted to expand itself from seven members to a maximum of twenty-five. They also voted to drop the

These Nursing students are gathered in Austin Hall in 1956, then the headquarters of Villanova's Nursing program. *Courtesy of Villanova University Archives*

requirement, in place since the beginning of Villanova's corporate existence, that members of the Board must be members of the Roman Catholic faith. The change was made so that the university could qualify for public funds, as well as tap the skills and influences of a wider population.

It was also in 1968 that Villanova opened all its programs to women for the first time. In reality, coeducation had come gradually over a period of fifty years, beginning with the summer school for nuns during World War I. In 1953 the College of Nursing had brought increasing numbers of women onto campus. Meanwhile, the daughters of faculty members were admitted to a variety of programs. By the late 1980s almost half the students at the university were women.

The year that Villanova expanded its board and admitted women to all its programs—1968—was also a year of upheaval in the United States. Both Martin Luther King, Jr., and Robert F. Kennedy were assassinated that year, and growing opposition to the Vietnam War forced President Lyndon B. Johnson not to seek another term in the White House. Riots and demonstrations also rocked the nation's cities and college campuses. These tides rolled over Villanova University and helped to exacerbate a growing discontent among its students.

Student unrest at Villanova began about 1965 and reached a peak in 1974, after which it quickly subsided. Although students involved in protests were in a distinct minority, they captured great attention.

Much of their discontent focused on the War in Vietnam, an increasingly unpopular conflict in which few students—at Villanova or elsewhere—wanted to

Students relax under a tree on an autumn afternoon at Villanova University. *Photograph by Peter Finger, 1991*

Reverend Robert J. Welsh, O.S.A., S.T.D., was President of Villanova University from 1967 to 1971. *Courtesy of Villanova University Archives*

Graduating senior, 1972. *Courtesy of Villanova University Archives*

Villanova students demonstrated outside administrative offices in Tolentine Hall on 7 February 1974. *Courtesy of Villanova University Archives*

fight. In November 1967 Villanova students demonstrated against recruiters from Dow Chemical, a producer of chemical weapons, and in January 1970 they targeted recruiters from General Electric because of its large defense contracts. Following President Richard Nixon's order to invade Cambodia in May of that year a wide array of campus organizations joined to publish an open letter to President Nixon in the *New York Times*. It was also in 1970 that a vocal group of Villanovans demanded that the NROTC unit leave campus.

Other protests arose from discontent with conditions at Villanova itself. In 1967 and 1969 there were riots in the Dougherty Hall dining room where students objected to the poor quality of the food. In 1967, and for some time thereafter, they criticized the university bookstore for carrying only textbooks. Still other protests focused on compulsory religious retreats, penalties for cutting classes, freshman hazing, irrelevant courses, and inadequate facilities in the student center (Dougherty Hall). But what infuriated students most was their seeming inability to influence university policy and the administration's refusal to allow visitation (or parietals) between male and female students in residence halls (as the university now called its dormitories).

The parietal question provoked several large "sit-ins" at women's residence halls, as well as demonstrations against the Board of Trustees which opposed visitations. In order to demand more of a voice in university policy hundreds of students occupied Tolentine Hall, the administrative center of the university, in February 1974.

The occupation of Tolentine Hall turned out to be the last of the large demonstrations on campus. After that protests began to subside, in part because students obtained much of what they wanted. They received a Student Bill of Rights in 1975 and limited visitation privileges in 1979. (The first co-ed residence hall opened in 1987, with male and female students housed on separate floors.) Compulsory retreats and religious services came to an end by 1970. Freshman hazing also ceased around 1970. The university agreed to build a new and much larger student center in 1976. The creation of a University Senate in 1970, which gave both students and faculty

more of a voice in decision making, further diffused tension. The end of the Vietnam War in 1974 also had a calming influence on Villanova, as well as on other campuses.

Student activism did not disappear completely after the mid-1970s, but it was less confrontational. In 1979 students marched for traffic safety after two students were injured, one by a car on Spring Mill Road and one by a SEPTA train. This action led to the installation of a traffic light between Saint Mary's Hall and the Law School, as well as improvements to the pedestrian tunnel under the railroad tracks, where constant flooding had forced students to use the bridge on Spring Mill Road or to try to walk across the tracks.

The upheavals of the 1960s and 1970s may have also led to greater concern for disadvantaged groups. Beginning in the late 1970s, Villanova hosted a segment of the Special Olympics. In the 1970s Balloon Day became a special event each spring. The courtyard outside Connelly Center was filled with game booths and concession stands, brightly decorated with bunches of helium-filled balloons. There were also rock bands and other entertainments. The event's sponsor, Campus Ministry, used the proceeds to fund various programs. Among its activities was an annual trip to Central America, where Villanova students helped to build housing in poor neighborhoods.

Greater sensitivity to minority groups also led the university to try to increase its enrollment of minority students. As an expression of its concern over apartheid in South Africa, the university decided to divest itself of companies doing business in that country.

Guest speakers during the past quarter-century addressed themselves to many issues. Reverend Philip Berrigan, S.J., the well-known anti-war protester, spoke at Villanova in 1968 and again in 1973. Professional organizer, Saul Alinsky, came in 1968. New Left advocate Tom Hayden appeared twice, in 1969 and 1972, the second time accompanied by actress and antiwar advocate, Jane Fonda. In 1970 championship boxer, Muhammed Ali, made an appearance, and in 1974 liberal anthropologist, Margaret Mead, lectured at the Field House.

The pages of *The Villanovan* crackled with student concerns. Throughout the 1960s and 1970s there were articles about black civil rights, women's rights, the environment, and, of course, the Vietnam War. By 1979 the newspaper was running stories on the Iranian hostage crisis. The 1980s brought alarm over smoking, acid rain, abortion, nuclear weapons, and AIDS. Another subject of discussion was underaged drinking and alcoholism, one which came up on many college campuses at the time.

The Villanovan also continued to devote space to political subjects, especially during the visits of prominent politicians. President Gerald R. Ford made a speech at Villanova during his campaign in 1976,

Reverend Edward J. McCarthy, O.S.A., Ph.D., was President of Villanova University from 1971 to 1975. *Courtesy of Public Relations*

Gerald Ford, President of the United States, visited Villanova during the presidential campaign on 27 October 1976. *Courtesy of Villanova University Archives*

George Bush, presidential contender, addressed a crowd of five hundred in the Connelly Center on 21 April 1980. *Courtesy of Villanova University Archives*

Students assist with the Special Olympics held annually at Villanova. *Courtesy of Student Activities, 1991*

and future President George Bush spoke on campus during his unsuccessful primary battle against Ronald Reagan in 1980. In 1988 Senator George McGovern, the Democratic presidential nominee in 1972, delivered an address at Villanova.

After favoring the Democrats in presidential elections for the past four decades, Villanova students switched to the Republicans in the 1970s. There is no evidence of a student poll in 1968, but in 1972 students favored Republican Richard M. Nixon over Democrat George McGovern. Republican Gerald R. Ford received twice the support of Democrat Jimmy Carter in 1976. In 1980 it was Republican Ronald Reagan over Carter by an equally large margin. There appears to have been no student poll in 1984, but in 1988 Republican George Bush rolled over Democrat Michael Dukakis by better than two to one. There were several reasons for this change to Republicanism, the most important being a growing affluence among Villanova parents.

By the mid-1960s students started coming to campus several weeks earlier than they did before—in late August or early September instead of mid to late September—because of the adoption of the "short semester" system. This allowed final

Balloon Day, painted by Brother Patrick Bohmann, O.S.A., portrays an event which first took place in 1973. Bohmann was a native of Cloppenburg, Germany, who spent twenty-nine years at the Monastery of Saint Thomas of Villanova as a gardener and sacristan. He took up painting at age seventy-five. His works are characterized by a charming simplicity and vivid colors. Brother Patrick died on the feast of Saint Thomas of Villanova, 22 September 1984. *Courtesy of Reverend Kail C. Ellis, O.S.A., Ph.D., Dean of the College of Liberal Arts and Sciences*

exams for the first semester to take place just before Christmas, thus eliminating the need to face them after the holiday break. Since classes for the second semester now ended in late April or early May, it also meant that students missed much of the spring season on campus, one of the favorite times of the year for prior generations of Villanovans. One casualty was Mother's Day, observed on campus since the mid-1930s. Yet another was Junior Week, a Villanova tradition which had been held during the second week in May for more than four decades.

Since Indian summer often lingered into early December, students now experienced a warm first semester, followed by a cold winter term. Frigid temperatures and record snowfalls in the late 1970s and early 1980s underlined these extremes. Heavy snows in February of 1978 and 1979 paralyzed the campus for several days, and in February 1983 Villanova experienced its largest snowfall ever—21.3 inches.

In 1981 Villanovans lost their intercollegiate football program, which was dropped by the Board of Trustees in 1981 because of its high costs. The alumni protested loudly and sponsored a benefit at Philadelphia's Academy of Music, featuring long-time celebrity Bob Hope. In late 1983 the trustees voted to restore football, though the first game was not played until November 1984. The following spring the campus was electrified when the Wildcat Basketball team won the NCAA championship at Louisville, Kentucky on 1 April 1985.

Two legendary figures of Villanova athletics passed from the scene in the 1980s. In 1981 James Francis "Jumbo" Elliott died. During his forty-seven years with Villanova he had coached twenty-eight Olympic contenders and had made Villanova's track teams famous all over the country. Four years later, in 1985, Villanova lost John "Jake" Nevin, who had been a trainer in the athletic program for thirty-six years.

Enrollments continued to rise in the 1970s and 1980s, though not so rapidly as they did in the 1960s. In 1971, for example, total enrollment was approximately 10,000, including the law school, graduate schools, the traditional undergraduate programs, and what was then called the Part-Time Division (later University Col-

Brother Patrick Bohmann, O.S.A., paints in his room at Saint Thomas of Villanova Monastery. *Courtesy of Villanova University Archives*

Reverend John M. Driscoll, O.S.A., Ph.D., was President of Villanova University from 1975 to 1988. *Courtesy of Public Relations*

Students of diverse backgrounds use the Reference Room of the Villanova College Library (now Falvey Hall) in 1967. *Courtesy of Villanova University Archives*

lege). In 1992 total enrollment was approximately 11,300. A decision in the 1980s to limit each freshman class to about 1,500 students slowed the university's growth. One reason for doing so was the shortage of housing on campus and the irritation of surrounding neighbors at having to put up with noisy students who lived off-campus.

Another reason for limiting undergraduate admissions was to assure rising SAT scores at a time when applications to the university were increasing. This idea of raising admissions requirements had been proposed fifty years earlier, but the Great Depression and World War II had made it impossible to fulfill. After the war a desperate need for higher education by returning servicemen and then the baby boom generation had led to a further postponement.

Orientation is just the beginning of what Villanova has to offer to its students. Every aspect of Villanova is highlighted for the incoming students including all activities, programs and that ever-present "Wildcat Spirit." The twin spires of Saint Thomas of Villanova Church soar in the distance in this Southwest Campus scene. *Photograph by Alan Nyiri*

In order to provide more and better facilities for its students and faculty, Villanova continued to erect new buildings. In 1968 it opened a new wing to the university library and a new bookstore and office building called Kennedy Hall. A large addi-

New students join hands to form a huge circle, one of many activities which take place during orientation. *Photograph by Alan Nyiri, 1991*

A few of the members of Villanova's sororities and fraternities strike a casual pose on an early spring day. *Photograph by Peter Finger, 1992*

tion to the Chemical Engineering Building opened in 1974. All three structures were rendered in a contemporary style. In order to house more students on campus the university erected, between the late 1960s and the late 1980s, a half dozen residence halls on a new South Campus, where the old college pond had once provided for ice skating and the setting for numerous tugs of war. All these buildings were designed in a contemporary style and faced in red brick, a total departure from the grey stone of the main campus.

A long awaited new university facility, the Connelly Center, opened in 1980. Resembling a ski lodge on the inside, the Connelly Center's peaked roofs blended

Commencement is always a festive time at Villanova, enlivened by the NROTC color guard and the orchestra. *Photograph by Alan Nyiri, 1991*

Photograph by Peter Finger, 1992

Villanova Women's Glee Club, the oldest women's organization in existence within the university, was founded in 1960 and originally comprised of twenty women from the College of Nursing. *Photograph by Alan Nyiri, 1991*

Graduation is an opportunity to thank parents, family, and friends for their love and support. *Photograph by Alan Nyiri, 1991*

well with the older Gothic motifs on campus. In 1986 the old Villanova Field House was superseded by the large Du Pont Pavilion, which gave the university the most modern athletic facilities available at the time, including a large Olympic-size swimming pool. The Pavillion's pointed, tent-like projections also blended well with older buildings. As the Sesquicentennial year begins, the new Saint Augustine Center for the Liberal Arts has opened. With its cross, dome, and steeply pitched gables it blends well with the Villanova landscape.

The rising quality of Villanova's faculty, physical plant, and student body won praise for the university. In 1985 Villanova received approval for a much coveted Phi Beta Kappa Chapter. That same year (25 November 1985) *U.S. News and World Report* rated Villanova the "No. 1" comprehensive university in the East. Five years later, in its issue for 15 October 1990, the same magazine described Villanova as "one of America's best colleges."

Villanova's Sesquicentennial celebration gives the university an excellent opportunity to explore the present and future through the perspective of the past. The marking of 150 years also provides an ideal atmosphere for comprehensive planning. These plans already include a major capital campaign; the strengthening of Villanova's core curriculum; the development of a West Campus; the construction of new residence halls; the renovation and restoration of Saint Thomas of Villanova Church; the continued pursuit of academic excellence; and, most importantly, a reaffirmation of Villanova's Augustinian ideals and Catholic character, combined with a commitment to greater cultural diversity. Villanova is well on its way to an even more glorious future.

Alumni Weekend, traditionally held in June, is time to rekindle old friendships, to recall the past and share fond memories of Villanova days. *Photograph by Alan Nyiri, 1991*

Saint Thomas of Villanova Church is in the center and Saint Rita's is on the right in this snow scene at Villanova University in the 1970s. *Courtesy of Public Relations*

Villanova Wildcat Basketball Team. *Photograph by Alan Nyiri, 1991*

Coaches Roland V. Massimino and Jay Wright throw themselves enthusiastically into the game. *Photograph by Alan Nyiri, 1992*

President Ronald Reagan welcomes the NCAA championship team to the White House following their victory on 1 April 1985. *Courtesy of Villanova University Archives*

Jumbo Elliott Track was dedicated on 27 September 1980 to James F. Elliott. Through long and faithful service to Villanova, he established a tradition of excellence in the sport of track and field, bringing international recognition and honor. *Photograph by Alan Nyiri, 1991*

Shelly Pennefather, seen playing on 30 March 1987, finished her basketball career as Villanova's all-time leading scorer for either men or women with 2,408 points. Shelly is now a member of the Order of Saint Clare, a cloistered community. *Courtesy of Sports Information*

The 1957 Villanova track team. Front row from left are Ed Collymore, Ron Delany, Coach Jumbo Elliott, Alex Breckenridge, and Charles Jenkins. Back row from left are Phil Reavis, Charlie Stead, and Don Bragg. Jenkins, Delany, and Bragg were Olympic gold medalists. Breckenridge and Reavis were also Olympians. *Courtesy of Sports Information*

Ron Delany, who was coached by "Jumbo" Elliott, kneels in prayer after winning a gold medal and securing a new Olympic record in the 1,500-meter run at the 1956 Summer Games in Melbourne, Australia. Australia's John Landy, who ran third, bends over Delany. *Courtesy of Public Relations*

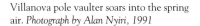

Olympic contender Vicki Huber, 1989. *Courtesy of Public Relations*

Villanova pole vaulter soars into the spring air. *Photograph by Alan Nyiri, 1991*

Students play volleyball on Mendel Field. The dome of Alumni Hall glows in the background. *Photograph by Alan Nyiri, 1991*

Gary Scott at bat, 1989. *Courtesy of Sports Information*

Jake Nevin, Villanova's veteran trainer, proudly wears the basketball net following the Wildcat's 66–64 upset over Georgetown University for the NCAA championship, 1 April 1985. Villanova's 1984–85 basketball season was dedicated to him. In 1984 he was inducted into the Big 5 Hall of Fame. Two months later the university retired "jersey number one," in Nevin's honor. *Courtesy of Public Relations*

A fast-moving soccer match at Villanova.
Photograph by Alan Nyiri, 1991

The Awakening, an abstract sculpture
donated by artsit Jay Dugan, greets students
as they make their way through campus.
The dome of Alumni Hall peaks through
the trees. *Courtesy of Alan Nyiri, 1991*

Reverend Bernard A. Lazor, O.S.A., S.S.L., is Chaplain to men's basketball, football, and the Alumni Association. Father Lazor strikes a familiar pose on the playing field. *Photograph by Alan Nyiri, 1991*

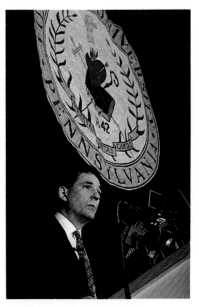

Steve Lappas, Villanova's new basketball coach, on 14 April 1992. *Courtesy of Sports Information*

Falvey Memorial Library, designed by architects Albert F. Dagit and Associates, was named for Reverend Daniel P. Falvey, O.S.A., M.S.L.S., Librarian from 1935 to 1962. This library, constructed in 1967, incorporates the earlier library, Falvey Hall, begun in 1947. *Photograph by Peter Finger, 1992*

Student in Falvey Memorial Library with Alumni Hall in background. *Photograph by Alan Nyiri, 1991*

Student studying in residence hall room. *Photograph by Alan Nyiri, 1991*

The 1974 addition to the Chemical Engineering Building was designed by architect Howell Lewis Shay, Jr. *Photograph by Peter Finger, 1992*

Connelly Center, designed by architects Vincent G. Kling and partners, was dedicated on 21 September 1980. His Eminence John Cardinal Krol, D.D., Archbishop of Philadelphia, presided at the dedication. A commemorative plaque in the President's Lounge reads, "May this center serve as a constant tribute to Josephine and John Connelly whose vision, spirit, and concern have enabled them to enrich the lives of so many." *Photograph by Alan Nyiri, 1991*

Belle Air Terrace, Connelly Center. 1991. *Photograph by Alan Nyiri, 1991*

Ground was broken for the DuPont Pavilion, designed by architects Daniel F. Tully and Associates, in the fall of 1983. The opening ceremonies took place on 1 February 1986 at which time the 1985 NCAA basketball champions defeated the University of Maryland, 64–62. The student population was then about 10,000. *Photograph by Alan Nyiri, 1991*

Former Presidents of Villanova University posed with Reverend Edmund J. Dobbin, O.S.A., S.T.D., after his Inaugural Mass on 5 October 1988. Together they spanned forty-four years of campus history. Left to right are Reverend Francis X. N. McGuire, O.S.A., D.D. (1944–1954); Reverend John M. Driscoll, O.S.A., Ph.D. (1975–1988); Father Dobbin (1988–Present); Reverend Robert J. Welsh, O.S.A., S.T.D. (1967–1971); and Reverend Edward J. McCarthy, O.S.A., Ph.D. (1971–1975). *Courtesy of Public Relations.*

The groundbreaking ceremony for the Liberal Arts Center was on 11 December 1990. Left to right are Reverend Kail C. Ellis, O.S.A., Ph.D., Dean, Liberal Arts and Sciences; Reverend Edmund J. Dobbin, O.S.A., S.T.D., President; Mr. James A. Drobile, Esq., Chairperson, Board of Trustees; and Reverend John J. Hagen, O.S.A., Ph.D., Augustinian Provincial, Province of Saint Thomas of Villanova. *Courtesy of Villanova University Archives*

Saint Augustine Center for the Liberal Arts, designed by architects Ueland, Junker and McCauley, was the fifty-fifth building on campus. *Photograph by Peter Finger, 1992*

NASA Astronaut Andrew M. Allen, Villanova 1977, spent four years in the Navy ROTC program and graduated with a degree in Mechanical Engineering. On 31 June 1992 Astronaut Allen piloted the Space Shuttle *Atlantis* in a complex scientific mission lasting approximately one week. *Courtesy of NASA*

Mrs. Denyse Lemaire-Ronveaux of the Geography Department explains a topographic map and a topographic profile. *Photograph by Peter Finger, 1991*

Reverend Arthur B. Chappell, O.S.A., S.T.D., explains the chalice, a sacred vessel used for liturgy, in a Religious Studies class. *Photograph by Peter Finger, 1991*

U.S. News & World Report, 15 October 1990, rated Villanova University as "one of America's best colleges." *Courtesy of Public Relations*

Doctor James W. Klingler teaches a class in management. *Photograph by Peter Finger, 1992*

(Opposite page) Villanova was approved for a much coveted Phi Beta Kappa Chapter in 1985, as a testament to its excellence in arts and sciences. *Courtesy of Honors Program*

PHI BETA KAPPA

founded *Dec.ʳ 5, 1776.*
Williamsburg, *Virginia.*

ΦΙΛΟΣΟΦΙΑ ΒΙΟΤ ΚΤΒΕΡΝΗΤΗΣ

C H A R T E R

To

Steven M. Amgott	Gerald J. Flood	Lucy McDiarmid
Earl D. Bader	Alan Gluchoff	Leon C. Robbins, Jr.
James O. Brooks	Don Goelman	Vincent B. Sherry
Michael E. Burke	Frederick W. Hartmann	Robert Styer
Edward L. Cannan	John Immerwahr	Deborah A. Thomas
Fred Carrier	Robert T. Jantzen	William D. Valente
Margaret A. Crouch	Brian J. Jones	William Werpehowski
William M. Fleischman	Deborah A. Kendzierski	Ellen Wertheimer

Members of ΦΒΚ *Greeting.*

WHEREAS, the liberal principles of our Society should not be confined to any particular place, Men or Description of Men, but should be extended to the wise and virtuous of whatever community;

WHEREAS, we, the Members of Φ Β Κ, as a body dedicated from its very founding in the historic year one thousand seven hundred and seventy-six at the College of William and Mary in Virginia to the ideal of excellence in scholarship in the liberal arts and sciences, are willing and desirous to propagate the Society in praiseworthy institutions of higher learning; and

WHEREAS, we are satisfied that you are inspired by an unquenchable desire that your institution be added to the notable company which enjoy the recognition of Φ Β Κ, and we have carefully determined that your institution is possessed of the character and standing which make it particularly worthy of admittance into this association and friendship;

Therefore, by virtue of a resolution duly adopted by our representatives in the thirty-fourth triennial Council of the United Chapters of Phi Beta Kappa, we have decreed the establishment at this time of a chapter of Φ Β Κ in Villanova University in the State of Pennsylvania, to be known as the Sigma of Pennsylvania.

FURTHERMORE, we have commanded that there issue under the seal of the Society and the hands of the President and the Secretary this Charter in the name of Φ Β Κ.

Accordingly, you and such others as you may hereafter elect and associate with yourselves in conformity to the law of Φ Β Κ, and your and their successors so elected and associated, are hereby incorporated and established as a separate and co-ordinate branch of the Society and are hereby granted all the powers, privileges, and benefits thereunto appertaining, in as full and ample measure as the members of the existing chapters enjoy: there being at the same time enjoined upon and required of you, in the organization and conduct of the Chapter and as conditions upon which this Charter is granted, strict compliance with the Constitution and By-Laws of the United Chapters of Phi Beta Kappa, with the acts of the Council and the Senate, and with the Chapter Constitution herewith transmitted to you; and likewise a devoted effort always to protect the name and key of Φ Β Κ from imitation and indignities and faithfully to promote the purposes of the Society.

In Testimony Whereof, the President and the Secretary of the United Chapters of Phi Beta Kappa have hereunto set their hands and caused to be affixed its seal this thirteenth day of April, *anno Domini* one thousand nine hundred and eighty-six.

Kenneth M. Greene
SECRETARY.

Norman F. Ramsey
PRESIDENT.

Alumni Hall as seen through the archway of
Corr Hall. *Photograph by Peter Finger, 1991*

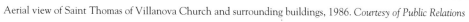
Aerial view of Saint Thomas of Villanova Church and surrounding buildings, 1986. *Courtesy of Public Relations*

Farrell Hall, acquired in 1978, is part of the former Morris Estate on Villanova's West Campus. Formerly called "Dundale," the mansion was designed in 1890 by architect Addison Hutton. The structure will be preserved as part of the development of the West Campus. *Courtesy of Villanova University Archives*

Saint Thomas of Villanova Church, built in the Victorian Gothic style, has been the center of spiritual life on the Villanova campus for over a century. It was designed by architect Edwin F. Durang and constructed between 1883 and 1887. The most notable stained glass window in the building is the resplendent representation of Saint Thomas of Villanova set above the church's front doorways. This and the other stained glass windows in the building were donated by several Augustinian parishes in the Philadelphia area and by two New York parishes, Saint Joseph in Greenwich and Immaculate Conception in Hoosick Falls. *Courtesy of Villanova University Archives*

Renovation and restoration of Saint Thomas of Villanova Church began in May 1991. Here a workman is laying white Carrera marble (Italy) and pink Saint Florient marble (Portugal). *Photograph by Alan Nyiri, 1991*

This workman is laying Stanstead gray granite (Canada) on the exterior of Saint Thomas of Villanova Church. *Photograph by Alan Nyiri, 1991*

Cross of Saint Thomas of Villanova Church silhouetted against the evening sky. *Photograph by Alan Nyiri, 1991*

Here rest generations of Augustinians whose legacy and spirit live on at Villanova and show the way to the future. *Photograph by Alan Nyiri, 1991*

Opposite page:
The twin spires of Saint Thomas of Villanova Church are among the most impressive sites on campus and symbolize Villanova University to the surrounding community. They were the basis for the Sesquicentennial Logo. *Photograph by Alan Nyiri, 1991*

Villanova University's Sesquicentennial Logo.

MESSAGE FROM THE PRESIDENT

I have chosen to place this brief message at the end of the photographs and texts which have detailed our history so that Janus-like, having reviewed the past, we might turn our face in hope and confidence to the future.

What we have seen provides us with strong and unmistakable evidence that over the past 150 years Villanova has been served generously, even nobly, by almost countless individuals who have made up her faculty, students, staff, alumni, parents, benefactors, friends—all who in some way or another have hailed her as ALMA MATER. In them was our beginning, a kind of leap of faith, which has evolved into the Villanova we know today. I speak of a continuum of ideals and hard work, first and foremost to provide the best education possible with the means at hand.

Today we look at a Villanova which seems so very different on the surface, but which has sought to maintain and strengthen the Catholic and Augustinian foundation and character while moving forward with the times. Within our framework of the Liberal Arts and Sciences we continue our tradition of the love of learning and the excitement of discovery while preparing students for eminent success in many walks of life. We have striven relentlessly to seek that living truth in the unity of the love which sustains us.

With the support which our past provides and the excitement of our present, we look forward to the future with confidence in God who sustains us and who, we trust, with the loving energy of our successors will bring this university of ours to even greater heights for the good of Villanovans in the future.

Reverend Edmund J. Dobbin, O.S.A., S.T.D.
President, Villanova University

Reverend Edmund J. Dobbin, O.S.A., S.T.D., thirty-first President of Villanova University. Inaugurated on 5 October 1988. *Photograph by Peter Finger*

ACKNOWLEDGMENTS

We are grateful for the encouragement and support of Reverend Edmund J. Dobbin, O.S.A., President of Villanova University; Reverend John J. Hagen, O.S.A., Augustinian Provincial, Province of Saint Thomas of Villanova; and Reverend George F. Burnell, O.S.A., Prior, Saint Thomas of Villanova Monastery.

We wish to thank the following individuals for their generous advice: D. M. Howe; Reverend Neil J. McGettigan, O.S.A.; Reverend Joseph C. Schnaubelt, O.S.A.; Reverend Joseph L. Shannon, O.S.A.; and Reverend Arthur Smith, O.S.A.

The Pictorial History Committee was helpful in many ways. Its members were Robert J. Casey; Sally Christ; David R. Contosta; Reverend Dennis J. Gallagher, O.S.A.; Frank Henninger; D. M. Howe; Donald B. Kelley; Christine A. Lysionek; Reverend Neil J. McGettigan, O.S.A.; and Reverend Joseph C. Schnaubelt, O.S.A.

Mary Ann Griffin, Director of Falvey Memorial Library, provided numerous resources for the authors. A member of her staff, Loretta Stango, cheerfully and proficiently typed various portions of the text.

Assisting with the photographs were Betsy Bobbitt, Thomas L. Davies, Adam F. Kelly, and Vincent J. Massa.

Christine A. Lysionek, Managing Director of the Sesquicentennial, encouraged and sustained the authors throughout this project. We give her special thanks.

The authors would also like to acknowledge the photographic work of the following individuals:

Peter Finger is a photojournalist, landscape photographer, and educator, who frequently travels on assignment to capture America on film. Each year, he photographs twenty colleges and universities, and his work is featured in books, magazines and calendars. He resides in Glenmont, New York

Alan Nyiri is one of the country's best-known campus photographers, having created images and photographic publications for more than two hundred colleges and universities. He has published numerous books containing landscape and nature studies of his native New England. When he is not on location, he resides in an old Vermont farmhouse with his wife, a college professor.

BIBLIOGRAPHY

"An Inside Story." Villanova, Penn.: Villanova College, 1930.

Annual Reports of Villanova University (1963–).

The Belle Air (yearbook), (1922–1992).

The Blue Book (student handbook). Villanova, Penn.: Villanova University, (1977–).

Breslin, Richard D. *Villanova: Yesterday and Today.* Villanova, Penn.: Villanova University Press, 1972.

Catalogues and Bulletins of Villanova College and University (1872–).

Commencement Addresses, (1852–).

Commencement Programs, (1853–).

Contosta, David R. and Gallagher, O.S.A., Reverend Dennis J. *Villanova, College to University: 150 years of Augustinian Tradition and Promise,* Villanova, Penn.: Villanova University Press, 1992. (catalogue)

The Directory of Villanova Alumni. White Plains, N.Y.: B. C. Harris Publishing Company (1973–).

Faculty Handbooks (1960–).

"For God and Country." Villanova, Penn.: Villanova College, 1930.

Graduate School Newsletter. Villanova, Penn.: Villanova University (1960–).

Men of Heart. Villanova, Penn.: Augustinian Press, 1983, 1986. 2 volumes.

Middle States Evaluation, 1970, 1990.

Middleton, O.S.A., Thomas C. *A Historical Sketch of the Augustinian Monastery, College, and Mission of St. Thomas of Villanova.* Villanova, Penn.: Villanova University Press, 1893.

____. Journals, 1865–1923. 2 volumes.

Minutes of the Board of Trustees, Villanova College and University (1848–).

Miller, Craig A. *The Year of the 'Cat. Villanova's Incredible NCAA Basketball Championship Story.* Villanova, Penn.: Villanova University Athletic Department, 1985.

Nite-Line. A Newsletter for the University College Student. (1979–).

O'Donnell, O.S.A., Michael J. *Villanova University Basketball, a Statistical History.* Villanova, Penn., 1962.

____. *Villanova University Football, a Statistical History.* Villanova, Penn.: Villanova University Press, 1964.

Orientation Newsletter. (1977–).

Parent's Connection (Parent's Newsletter). (1984–).

Philadelphia Inquirer. *'Nova No. 1.* Indianapolis, Ind.: News Books International, 1985.

Radan, George T. *Villanova University Art Collection; a Guide.* Villanova, Penn.: Villanova University, 1986.

Reflections. Villanova, Penn.: Villanova University (1975–1980, 1985–).

Report to the President by the Program Evaluation Committee, Volumes 1–6, 1988.

Report of the Inspection of Villanova College by an Evaluating Committee of the Middle States Association of Colleges and Secondary Schools, 1950.

Report of Villanova University Submitted to Middle States Association of Colleges and Secondary Schools, 1960.

Reuschlein, Harold G. *The Villanova University School of Law.* Prospect, Ky.: Harmony House, 1991.

Special Report. A special briefing for trustees and trustee associates (1990–).

The Spires (1974–1984).

The Spires; Tolle Lege (1985–).

Stanford, O.S.A., Edward V. *A Guide to Catholic College Administration.* Westminster: The Newman Press, 1965.

Student's Handbook. Villanova, Penn.: Villanova College, 1931–1953.

Tourscher, O.S.A., Francis E. *Old Saint Augustine's in Philadelphia....* Philadelphia, Penn.: P. Reilly Company, 1937.

Track and Field Media Guide (1976–).

University News Bulletin. Villanova, Penn.: Villanova University, (1980–1984).

Varsity Club Newsletter (1979–).

Villanova Alumni Magazine (1968–1970).

Villanova Alumnus (1933–1936, 1938–1974).

Villanova Football Media Guide (1978–).

Villanova Magazine. Villanova, Penn.: Villanova University (1985–).

The Villanova Monthly. Villanova, Penn. (1893–1897).

"Villanova Shall Go Farther." Villanova, Penn.: Villanova College, 1930.

Villanova Student Activities Handbook (1965–1966–).

Villanova University Basketball Media Guide (1977–).

Villanova University Women's Basketball Media Guide (1983–).

Villanvoa Women's Athletic Guide (1982–1983).

Villanova Women's Sports Guide (1980–1982).

The Villanovan (student newspaper), (1916–).

Women's Track Media Guide (1983–).

INDEX

ABOUT THE AUTHORS

David R. Contosta, Ph.D., is Professor and Chair of the History Department at Chestnut Hill College in Philadelphia. He is also an adjunct faculty member in the History Department at Villanova University. He earned his doctorate in history from Miami University in 1973. Dr. Contosta is the author of eight books and numerous articles and reviews. These writings include biographies of Henry Adams and the Houston/Woodward families, urban and suburban history, architecture, historic preservation, oral history, and a variety of topics in social, cultural, and intellectual history, as well as the United States in the Gilded Age and twentieth century.

Dr. Contosta lectures widely to both professional and popular audiences and has served as a consultant to historical societies and museums in the greater Philadelphia area. In 1983–84, he was a Commonwealth Speaker for the Pennsylvania Humanities Council. He has held or participated in grants from the National Endowment for Humanities, the American Philosophical Society, and the Pew Foundation. In 1972–73, he was a Fulbright Fellow to France. Dr. Contosta has collaborated on Villanova's Sesquicentennial Historical Exhibit, is co-author of the exhibit catalogue, and of *Ever Ancient, Ever New*, a pictorial history of Villanova University. At present, he is writing a Sesquicentennial history of Villanova University. Dr. Contosta lives at Plymouth Meeting, Pennsylvania, with his wife Mary, who teaches Spanish at Villanova University. He is also the father of four children.

Reverend Dennis J. Gallagher, O.S.A., Ph.D., was ordained to the priesthood on 30 January 1965 at Saint Thomas of Villanova Church on the Villanova University campus. He is the Villanova University Archivist, a position which he has held since 1985. Father Gallagher earned his Ph.D. in Administration (Higher Education) from the Catholic University of America, Washington, D.C., in 1975. He also holds a master's degree in Religious Studies from Augustinian College, Washington, D.C., and a master's degree in Library Science from Villanova University. He received his undergraduate degree from Villanova in 1960.

Following ordination in 1965, he held teaching assignments at several Augustinian schools: Austin Preparatory School, Reading, Massachusetts, and Malvern Preparatory School, Malvern, Pennsylvania. After completing his doctorate in 1975, he was assigned to Villanova University in the Graduate School. He also serves as a Residence Hall Minister in Stanford Hall, Villanova University. In addition to his university responsibilities, Father Gallagher is involved in parish ministry. Presently he assists at Saint Catharine's and Saint Margaret's Parish in Spring Lake, New Jersey.

Father Gallagher was inducted into the Legion of Honor, the Chapel of the Four Chaplains, in 1984, for his service to community. He is also a member of the Knights of Columbus.

Father Gallagher has been actively involved in a variety of projects for Villanova's Sesquicentennial celebration. Most importantly, he is the Chairperson of the Historical Exhibits, "Villanova, College to University: 150 Years of Augustinian Tradition and Promise, 1842–1992." This exhibit will be on display in the Connelly Center during the anniversary year, September 1992 to September 1993. He is also co-author of the exhibit catalogue, and of *Ever Ancient, Ever New*, a pictorial history of Villanova University.

VILLANOV

JULY